It's a Shrinking Business!

How to Run a Psychiatric Practice

Danny Allen

Cartoon and cover design by Robbie Mills

It's a Shrinking Business

Copyright © 2014 Danny Allen

ISBN-13: 978-1497411708
ISBN-10: 149741170X

All Rights Reserved. No part of this publication may be reproduced in any form or by any means, including scanning, photocopying, or otherwise without prior written permission of the copyright holder.

Disclaimer and Terms of Use: The Author and Publisher has strived to be as accurate and complete as possible in the creation of this book, notwithstanding the fact that she does not warrant or represent at any time that the contents within are accurate due to the rapidly changing nature of the Internet. While all attempts have been made to verify information provided in this publication, the Author and Publisher assumes no responsibility for errors, omissions, or contrary interpretation of the subject matter herein. Any perceived slights of specific persons, peoples, or organisations are unintentional. In practical advice books, like anything else in life, there are no guarantees of income made. Readers are cautioned to rely on their own judgment about their individual circumstances to act accordingly. This book is not intended for use as a source of legal, business, accounting or financial advice. All readers are advised to seek services of competent professionals in the legal, business, accounting, and finance fields.

Dedication

This book is dedicated to the memory of

Dr David Bennett

Mentor, maverick and consummate businessman

It's a Shrinking Business

Other books by Danny Allen

We Need It By Next Thursday - The Joys of Writing Psychiatric Reports 2nd Edition 2014

Do You Know a Good Expert? - Lawyers Tell Psychiatrists What They Want (Editor) 2nd Edition 2014

Business for Medics – How to Set Up and Run a Medical Practice 2014

Contents

Foreword 7
Introduction 9
Chapter 1 - What will I do? 15
Chapter 2 - Setting up in business 25
Chapter 3 - Legal and professional matters 33
Chapter 4 - Creating time 39
Chapter 5 - Your workplace 45
Chapter 6 - Getting paid 51
Chapter 7 - Employing people 61
Chapter 8 - Expanding 71
Chapter 9 - Succession planning 81
Chapter 10 - Putting it into practice 87
Acknowledgements 101
We Need It By Next Thursday – The Joys of Writing Psychiatric Reports 103
Do You Know a Good Expert? - Lawyers Tell Psychiatrists What They Want 115
About The Author 139
Bibliography 141
Webography 143
Index 145

It's a Shrinking Business

Foreword

Picking this book up, means that you already have an interest, and some involvement, in private psychiatric practice. Private practice is great! The pleasure and pride in patients wanting to come and see you because of your reputation and skill, as opposed to being just a member of a Mental Health Trust team. That someone values your opinion so much, they are prepared to pay you a fee. The reward of being able to relate personally to a patient, without managers and teams being involved, and the pleasure of receiving a Christmas card and a bottle of wine, with a note of thanks, as opposed to yet having to justify your actions for detaining an unwilling patient, before a Mental Health Tribunal. Being involved in private practice gives you a greater sense of freedom and ability to distance yourself from problems of the modern NHS. It makes you feel more valued.

Medico-legal work is intellectually stimulating. It allows you the time to unravel complex clinical problems and to justify your opinion, sometimes under cross-examination. As your practice will inevitably grow, it is important to start this adventure off on a sound footing. This little book is a mine of helpful information on to how to avoid making mistakes and how to set up a good practice ripe for future expansion. Having run successful full-time private psychiatric practice myself for 15 years, there are still several points raised in this book, that I realised I needed to address!

Cosmo Hallström MD FRCP FRCPsych DPM

Consultant Psychiatrist

Introduction

Many psychiatrists think that all they have to do, in order to go into private or medico-legal practice, is to show willing and charge money. The truth, unsurprisingly, is much more complex. For a number of years now I have been going up and down the country, giving short talks and whole day workshops on how doctors should run their businesses and I thought it was about time that I put this into writing, to open it up to a bigger audience. It seemed appropriate, having written a book introducing psychiatrists to the joys of report writing and editing another one by lawyers, that this book should form the third of the trilogy.

This book draws on over twenty years' of experience; most of it found out either along the way or by making mistakes. Making mistakes is inevitable if you are making sufficient decisions - wise words from Pete Sudbury, my sometime medical director - but some mistakes can be too costly to contemplate and I heard quite a few horror stories from people in workshops, making me think that doctors really should learn a few things before they consider selling their services.

It's a Shrinking Business

The fact that you have bought (or borrowed) this book suggests a certain degree of insight; others all too frequently carry on blithely, unaware that what they are doing is unlawful. So far I have yet to hear of a doctor being prosecuted for a failure to have employer's liability insurance, but one often hears of doctors pursued by HMRC (Her Majesty's Revenue and Customs) for failure to pay sufficient tax and it is inevitable that, where this crosses the threshold for criminal prosecution, these doctors will find themselves referred to the GMC (General Medical Council).

In this book I hope you will not only learn about the basics of setting up a business, but also some of the 'tricks of the trade', useful for all doctors, not just psychiatrists. Similarly it is important that you are aware of some of the common pitfalls, particularly in those circumstances where you are in real danger of breaking the law if you do not know what you are doing. In my estimation, private practice and medico-legal work should be pleasurable, lawful and profitable; all three matter, more or less equally.

Another important issue, for UK doctors, is that the vast majority of us work in the NHS and whilst some may only start a practice on retirement, many more will want to run one in parallel. Indeed, even if you are planning to start after retirement, you will soon gather, on reading this book, that this is not something you should contemplate without a certain amount of planning, so if you are looking for a smooth transition from NHS to private practice, you may well be advised to start whilst you are still employed. Thus I will spend some time talking about how the rules governing NHS contracts in England, at least as they pertain to working privately.

So what can you expect from this book? Well, by the time you have finished it you should be in a good position to start your practice on a sound basis. First and foremost, you will have recognised that you are going into business. This may sound totally daft, but my experience suggests that this is not really something which most doctors think about. They think they are doing a bit of doctoring and that the business aspects are for someone else. That 'someone' may be the clinic they are in or the hospital whose consulting rooms they rent – just not them!

Like most other things in medicine it pays to 'read around' your subject. By having a working understanding of the laws and conventions which surround the world of business, you will be in a much better position to think of the things you need to be considering, even if they are new – and new rules are promulgated with monotonous regularity – so that even if everything you read here is not 100% up to date (and how could it be) you will know who to ask to find out the up to date situation. So, by the end of this book, I hope you will be able to:

- Understand why slipping your NHS secretary a tenner for typing a report is unlawful
- Know how to negotiate space for your practice in your job plan
- Realise that an accountant is worth their weight in gold
- Be able to confidently issue tax compliant invoices.
- Have a good understanding of your responsibilities in the business world
- Understand your extra professional responsibilities
- Make sure you train appropriately for your role
- Keep appropriate records
- Make sure you have a mentor or supervisor
- Always be ethical
- Create time to perform your role
- Be open with your employer
- Choose your workplace carefully

- Use modern tools to make yourself more available
- Understand how to employ people legally and ethically
- Use an outsourced payroll function
- Maintain good relationships with your customers
- Make sure you get paid
- Consider how to work with others
- Understand that your business has a value
- Network to get referrals/instructions
- Manage your time and delegate

I hope you enjoy reading this book and benefit from the information in contains. I apologise in advance for any inaccuracies. I have done my best to avoid them but in making the decision to write the book, I have inevitably opened myself up to the possibility that the odd one will slip in!

It's a Shrinking Business

Chapter 1 - What will I do?

Forgive me for putting this chapter in the book. If you know exactly what you are going to do and how you will do it, you may move straight to chapter 2. However, my experience of talking to people shows that doctors sometimes only have a very vague idea about what they want to do and, furthermore, how they might go about it. What am I talking about? Well, for example you may be a jobbing adult psychiatrist and think you want to do some private practice. However when you come to set up you realise that you rather like working with people with schizophrenia but that private practice does not enable you to see people with psychosis and, even if they are referred, you lack the necessary team structure to deal with these patients effectively.

Alternatively you might want nothing to do with psychosis in your private practice, considering that you want a complete change from what you do in the NHS. But you may not get referred many patients. So, if you are thinking of seeing private patients you may want to think of going into a niche area.

For doctors who like the idea of medico-legal work, they may think this is something they can just go straight into, but then find themselves embarrassed because they do not know how to compile a report, in particular because they do not know the rules which apply to their chosen field.

Private practice

Many psychiatrists run exclusively medico-legal practices (about which, more below), so deciding to see private patients is tantamount to making a choice – of course there is absolutely no reason why you should not do both but it is as well to think these things through because all choices have implications. First and foremost, as you will find out in chapter 5, is the issue of where you can see patients. You are definitely constrained as to planning permission and, if you do no **NHS** practice, **CQC** (Care Quality Commission) rules and therefore, if you do not want to see that many patients, you may well decide that your best option is to get practising privileges at a local private hospital (not necessarily psychiatric) for this purpose.

However, for the purposes of this section, I shall assume that you are very keen on seeing private patients. The first thing to consider is the likely 'market'. There are no real shortcuts. You may need to ask a lot of people, GPs, colleagues etc. and even then you may be none the wiser. At the end of the day you may just need to 'dip your toe in the water'. But this means that you cannot (unless you have lots of money saved) expend vast quantities of money on premises or even staff. Hence renting rooms of one sort or another is probably your best option.

Private practice depends, inevitably, on money. This money will come either straight out of the pockets of your patients or from private insurance. In either case, unless you happen to live in a community of lottery winners and landed gentry, this will depend on people being in employment - and a lot less will be in a recession. So being aware of external financial realities is probably as important as knowing who you want to be treating.

So, of course you can be a 'broad-spectrum' psychiatrist, but I suggest that it can be helpful to make known the areas of practice in which you have an 'interest', even if these are only those areas in which you think people will most need help – e.g. resistant depression and anxiety. Taking things a stage further, how about thinking about what is missing from the

NHS? What do people (GPs and patients) ask for but get denied? Obvious answers might include things like adult ADHD (Attention Deficit Hyperactivity Disorder), ASD (Autistic Spectrum Disorder) or mild dementia.

Giving some thought to such matters enables you to plan ahead and, where appropriate, train for your role. I would suggest that, if you want to invest in your future private practice, a two day training course on adult ADHD may be a better use of money, and, as you will discover in the next chapter, totally tax deductible, than renting medical chambers with no certainty of work.

Giving some thought to what you might like to do (and even training for the role) is only the beginning though, because some roles require you to 'partner' with others and though this may seem simple in theory my experience is that this is the point at which most schemes fall down. I have had numerous meetings with people who have brilliant ideas for 'services' but who do not have either the 'staying power' or the drive to make them come to fruition. These things are not for the faint-hearted, yet the concept of running a 'service' as opposed to just having a practice is very attractive, not only to the practitioners but also to patients and referrers. Well-run services should be able to both inspire confidence and deliver the goods but they take quite a lot of sustained effort to set up.

Medico-legal work

As anyone who has read either 'We Need It By Next Thursday or 'Do You Know a Good Expert?' will know, there is a huge field of medico-legal work out there for psychiatrists but, these days, unlike 'when I were a lad' one would be well-advised to prepare and train carefully for the role. Not that I am trying to put anyone off. On the contrary I believe it to be a very fulfilling role and one which I would encourage any young psychiatrist (and maybe even a few old ones) to get into. Just make sure you don't try to run before you can walk.

There are many courses, not least those run by Bond Solon, which exist to teach doctors about medico-legal work. At the point of writing there is no formal 'qualification' for being an expert, but there is a gentle pressure leading in this general direction and, in my book, wherever this is the case, it pays to get ahead of the game, even were it not a good idea in its own right.

It's a Shrinking Business

At the very least it is as well to be aware that there are rules governing the three main jurisdictions, civil, criminal and family and to go looking for them. These rules require certain wording on reports and, if you fail to include this, you are going to look like a rank amateur. Far better, though, to invest some money in going on a course introducing you to report-writing. If you can find someone who already does this sort of work, why not approach them for some support and mentoring? Most of us are only too keen to help colleagues.

Whatever you decide to do, it makes sense to start at the bottom and work your way up. Whilst you are unlikely to be asked to do a murder case without any prior experience, the odd naïve solicitor might just do so and you may feel your ego being stroked. Probably best to resist the temptation on day one!

Cases in the Magistrates' Courts are usually done by local solicitors who may well ask you to report. Sometimes this will be on people who are already your (NHS) patients. If this is the case there are two factors to consider. The first is whether you feel comfortable that there are no conflicts of interest preventing you from reporting – this will apply whether the patient is in the NHS or not. The second, applying only to

It's a Shrinking Business

NHS patients and to be covered in much greater detail in this book, is to make sure that you deal with any such request in a business-like way, at one remove from the NHS.

In the civil arena the obvious place to start is with personal injury cases involving road traffic accidents. Most of these are handled by agencies, so you can look for agencies active at the time you read this book. I use this phrase advisedly because these companies have a nasty habit of going out of business without so much as a 'by your leave. It pays to check them out and it pays to make sure you get a formal contractual agreement as to when you will be paid – and if you are not, to seriously consider suing them for any money owing before they go bankrupt. More of this below.

As I write, family court work – which used to provide me with a very good living – has all but dried up. Most of us 'in the game' think it will re-emerge, albeit in stilted form but it is a very salutary lesson indeed about the need for flexibility and diversification. The dramatic downturn is partially due to an enforcement of lower fees by the Ministry of Justice, but much more so by an enforced culture change, by that same ministry, which has allowed judges to take a much more assertive role in case management. Whilst we, as experts, may have our views (sometimes pretty trenchant) on our own utility, it matters not a whit if the judges think otherwise. Anyway this is not the place to rehearse the wide variety of other work available – read one or both of the other books referred to at the beginning of this section if you want to know more!

Other streams of work

What else might psychiatrists do? Well they may teach, they may write (including books!) and they may become **SOADs** (second opinion approved doctors) appraisers (of colleagues for revalidation purposes – a growing career choice!) or tribunal doctors. Some of these roles, at least, are clearly paid work but differ from pure employment by the discretion associated with the choice of working hours. Hence they fit well into a 'portfolio career'. Some colleagues feel very strongly that 'time is money' and demand payment for anything. You will have to decide where you sit on the spectrum. I have accepted money for lecturing when it is offered, for example, but I don't always insist on it.

By the way, don't expect to make much (if any) money from writing books! Unless you are a great academic (in which case still don't expect to be able to retire on the proceeds) you are likely, these days, to spend a small amount self-publishing, then struggle to recoup your costs. But it is really jolly good fun and you should not be put off if you feel the urge. It is great for filling in those gaps where work is slack, patients or clients don't show or that week between Xmas and New Year when everything closes down and you want to get away from the in-laws!

Some psychiatrists, particularly those who have left the NHS, like to combine self-employment with a part-time job. This is often an excellent option. Such jobs are sometimes available within the NHS to people after retirement; as a basic rule of thumb for people under 60 (where these rules apply) you can work for up to 2 days - 4PAs (professional activities) a week without a decrement in your pension. However, please do not *rely* on this book – rules change and you must always check these things with your pension provider. If you are lucky enough to get even one PA's work then (at the point of writing) you are absolved from having to register with the CQC for your private practice (see Chapter 8 for more detail). Again rules change so you must check the up to date situation. Substance misuse jobs in the private sector are often part-time and of course all sorts of other jobs exist. You may be asked to become a (non-executive) director of a charity involved with some area of medical practice. If you are tempted in this direction I would also advise you to train appropriately for the role – the Institute of Directors does some very good courses.

In this chapter we have looked at some of the choices available to psychiatrists who want to go into practice. The main two are private (medical) practice and medico-legal practice, and many will choose to do both together. Having the ability to diversify is important as external constraints may influence what is available at any point in time.

Chapter 2 - Setting up in business

In this chapter we will look at the basics of running a business – as this is what you are doing if you are working for money on your own account. The biggest mistake made by doctors is to not take this aspect of work seriously. It matters because there are certain laws which govern business behaviour and you ignore them at your peril.

The precontemplation stage

Most doctors, including even myself, will do some work for money before setting up as a business. The reason for this is obvious. Sometimes in life things creep up on us and catch us unawares. In my case I started a forensic job and was taught how to write reports. It was, of course, normal practice to ask for payment for these reports which had to be typed by someone and thus we were 'instructed' to pay the secretaries who typed them. For others, you might find yourself doing Mental Health Act assessments or, perhaps at an even earlier stage of your career, filling in 'crem forms'. The first thing to bear in mind is that, as long as you are simply being paid for something, you will remain on the right side of the law as long as you declare your earnings. However this is likely not to be the case once you pay someone else.

Also, the law allows you some leeway to register as self-employed after you have started earning money. The longer you leave it, though, the more advisable it is to get expert advice – certainly it is wise to do so if more than a year has passed. The key reason and, indeed, the main issue, which I hope you will appreciate as you read on, is that you are the loser if you simply declare your earnings. The taxman will be delighted to take 40% of everything you declare, no questions asked. The law allows you to keep some of this but, in order to do this you need to be accepted as a self-employed person. Secondly, as you will learn, double taxation in 'year one' is better done whilst you are still earning a pittance.

So, although many people find themselves being asked to do work before they have considered 'setting up', the sooner you do this the better and ideally you should do this, at your leisure, before you are earning 'serious money'. For psychiatrists I would suggest that this point will perhaps come once you are approved under Section 12(2) of the Mental Health Act 1983 and you contemplate doing some Mental Health Act assessments for which you will be paid. But it could come in other ways also and there is no harm in being prepared and declaring no income for a year or two. In the 'real world' many businesses (plan to) make losses in their first few years' trading anyway so a zero balance is absolutely fine and indeed you may think of some things you need to buy ahead of the time when you will earn money in order for you to do your work. What about a map-book or sat-nav to find those difficult addresses in the community for your Mental Health Act assessments, for instance?

The other issue to consider is the extent to which you want to 'go it alone'. I remembering going round to my friend's house when I was a medical student and his father, who by this time was a judge, gave me some sage advice: "Get an accountant before you need one". I would add that this accountant should be a good one - ask around amongst those who are well informed. Whilst this is advice I commend to you, many of the steps I will outline below you can do alone and may want to in the early days. That said, having the structure of having to report to an accountant is a good discipline and ultimately 'protective' against the ravages of the taxman - and you won't have to pay for the things you do yourself. 'Throwing' all your receipts at the accountant and expecting him or her to sort out your tax return is going to work out a hell of a lot more expensive - and probably not worth your while - compared with presenting him or her with a spreadsheet summarising your incomings and outgoings.

Starting a business

Firstly you need to register with HMRC as a business. Forms can easily be found online and you can do this retrospectively within the first year. You will need a name – even if it is as simple as Dr Bloggs Psychiatric Practice.

You need to be aware that you will be taxed double in your first year (you get this back when your business is wound up). This is an excellent reason for registering early – before you find this is too onerous. You need to decide on your accounting year. You can stick with the tax year but, if you are good at putting money aside, you may wish to consider one which finishes on, for example, April 30th. This means you have over a year to collect the money from your debtors before tax is due.

You also need to fill in an annual form to 'defer' national insurance contributions. This assumes you are already earning over the maximum contribution income with your employment. The term 'defer' actually means not paying any via your business because you have already paid it in your employment. If all this sounds complicated – get an accountant!

Running a business

You need to be 'business-like'. This means having some discipline in the way you conduct your affairs, like having a 'proper' invoicing system. You should have numbered sequential invoices, dated and signed by yourself or your representative. They should show a reliable trading address and give any information about the name of your business, particularly if they are issued under a trading name. They should state the nature of the service and when it was performed. You should have a way of collecting and recording what money you have collected. Cheap accounting systems are easy to come by but in the early days you can just use a numbered invoice system on an ordinary 'Word' document if you wish. Records have to be kept for at least 6 years in case HMRC audits your business.

The more you can do yourself, the less you need to pay an accountant for. At each stage of your expansion, think about whether it is cheaper to employ someone to do a task for you than to either spend your (relatively expensive) time or your accountant's possibly more expensive time. There is more information in Chapter 7 - about employing people.

From the start you need to get into the habit of documenting and keeping evidence of your expenses, to set off against your income; otherwise you will pay too much tax! So keep, in some sort of order, your receipts. Remember that anything associated with your business is fair game as can be parts of things you use for business. A list of categories is available on a standard self-employed tax return. Again you are best checking with an accountant who, in the early days at least, is likely to be able to offset the value of his or her fees with the money you can save!

Legal issues pertaining to business

The major issue in business (before you start employing people) is tax law. Unless you register as a business, and therefore get taxed under a self-employment regime, you only have two choices. The first is 'forget' to declare additional income. This is clearly unlawful and ultimately may be criminal. The second is to declare income as 'additional'. For very occasional amounts this may be fine but as you start earning more you will inevitably end up paying too much tax. This is because it is only by registering as a business/self-employed that you can claim expenses.

My advice is also to get a business account, to keep business earnings separate, with a deposit account to save for tax. In the event of any HMRC investigation will also demonstrate that you have kept a proper separation between business and personal finances meaning that there is less of a chance of the investigation 'bleeding' into other areas of your finances..

The business plan

Now, in a very ideal world, you will also make a business plan. The details of how to do this are outside the scope of this book, but at the very least it is a statement of what your business will do (or does), the competition, your marketing strategies and a strengths and weaknesses analysis of your approach with some mention of finances. If you ever need to get a significantly large business bank loan you will certainly need to do one of these but it is a useful discipline for yourself if you are really planning ahead. However, I don't want to labour this point as I appreciate that many people reading this book will not necessarily be ready for this level of structure at the beginning of their career, as they will still, effectively, be doing this type of work alongside their NHS work. If you feel that you are at a higher level of sophistication, I suggest that you might want to do a bit of further research into business practice.

In this chapter we have covered the basics of business. Firstly setting up by registering with HMRC, secondly organising yourself along business-like lines, keeping all receipts and recording all transactions. Having a business plan is a good idea if you are properly planning ahead and the importance of having an accountant from an early stage was emphasised, as was the danger, legally, of doing things improperly.

Chapter 3 - Legal and professional matters

In this chapter we will look at your duties and responsibilities as a professional and specifically as a doctor.

Data

Anyone who handles data must be registered under the appropriate category with the Information Commissioner's Office. You can find details online. It is also good practice to tell patients or clients about how you will be using their data (for admin, letters to GPs and reports for example). A good place to give this information is in their appointment letter. Please note that this is not something you can leave to any hospital where you see patients or clients. These days they will normally expect you to provide evidence that you are registered as a data controller in your own right.

You also need, as a data controller, to make sure that the data you hold is held securely. There is no prescription for exactly how you should do this but you need to take common-sense reasonable precautions. For example, locked filing cabinets and password-protected computers should be the norm. If you transport notes in your car, a locked briefcase and not leaving it in the car whilst you pop to the pub are sensible precautions.

If you do need to send documents by email, you should encrypt them – and make sure the password is agreed other than by an email sent just after or just before to the same email address as the document (a common practice which has no security value if you think about it). A verbally agreed password is one possible solution. Another is to agree passwords by email sent from the putative receiver's email to the putative sender's, at a completely separate time in advance.

Better still, there are a number of 'platforms' for uploading documents to 'the cloud' which can be password-protected and many, such as Google Drive, offer free means for storing files securely (assuming this term has some meaning post-Snowden). Google Drive, in particular, has a useful function for connecting to Google Calendar so that files can be connected to client or patient appointments and other data.

The notes of adult patients need to be kept for 20 years at least and even longer for children. Medico-legal notes have to be kept for 6-10 years. Keeping them in perpetuity (in a scanned archive) is one sensible option (see the Webography for details).

Medical Defence

You need to make sure that you are signed up with a medical defence organisation and that the level of your cover is appropriate for the work you do. There will usually be some sort of tariff for both private and medico-legal work. If there is a change in the amount you earn (or are likely to earn that year) you must inform them; this is not something you should put off. I would also suggest that you develop a low threshold for ringing them up and seeking advice about anything with which you are unfamiliar or uncertain. Prevention is always better than cure. You can also write to them with information about issues you feel have the potential to 'blow up' even when nothing has happened and they can keep the information on file.

Insurance

You need to consider what insurance you need. We will deal with employees below but the sorts of things you need to be thinking about include insurance of any premises you own or rent and their contents as well as public liability insurance. If you already have health-related income protection insurance, remember to extend it to your independent practice – or maybe this is the time to get advice from an Independent Financial Advisor (IFA). A particularly useful type of insurance you may not have heard of (unless you have an accountant) is tax investigation insurance in case HMRC decide to audit you. However well organised you are, a tax audit is time consuming and, if you are insured, that time (and associated expense) can be your accountant's.

Training and Supervision

Just like any new role you need to train for what you do. Whilst this may not be so relevant for private practice, it is absolutely vital, these days, that if you want to do any medico-legal work whatsoever, you understand what jurisdiction you are working in and get appropriately trained. There are lots of courses on the internet; Bond Solon is one example of a company which specialises in this sort of course. You don't want to make a fool of yourself because you did not know that you needed to put a particular prescribed 'Statement of Truth' on your report, for example. There are separate sets of rules, these days, for civil reports (the Civil Procedure Rules – CPR), criminal reports (the Criminal Procedure Rules CrPR) and family reports – you get the picture.

Continuing Professional Development (from a College and GMC viewpoint) needs to cover all aspects of your practice. You should choose (or re-choose) you peer group appropriately; you don't want to feel uncomfortable talking about your training needs with someone who thinks that training for your role equates only to training for your NHS job! If your Trust is one of those which tries to control who your peer group is then you may want to consider setting up a second group to address those needs. In any case meeting a group of colleagues, for example to have a case-based discussion around medico-legal reports is good practice. Finding a good mentor or supervisor is a good idea. Many people who have done this sort of work for years would be very willing to support you. Some charge; others don't – shop around.

In this chapter we covered the requirements all data handlers have to register with the Information Commissioner and to safeguard data. We looked at the specific responsibilities doctors have to be appropriately covered by their defence organisation, we considered what insurance one may need to take out and thought about the importance of appropriate training and supervision.

It's a Shrinking Business

Chapter 4 - Creating time

In this chapter we will look at the practicalities of setting up and running a practice at the same time as doing your NHS or other main role. We will consider the benefits of delegation and start thinking about how employing people to help you can assist in freeing up your time.

Job planning

In theory there is a very clear structure for consultants to plan their job within the NHS. Private organisations will have similar structures in place in some cases. In practice job planning in the NHS is more often observed in the breach. It is tempting to just get on with your private or medico-legal practice and not say anything. However, at the very least, when a job-planning meeting is arranged by your employer, you need to be completely up-front about what you are doing as a failure to do so will lead to questions about your probity being raised.

The so-called 'new' contract (possibly soon to become 'old'), which virtually all consultants will now be on, actually has a specific requirement with regard to private practice for full time (10 PA) consultants. In order to work privately one has to 'offer' the Trust a session of (paid) extra work. In practice, in psychiatry, this is often a legal fiction, as few psychiatric Trusts want you to work anymore than 10 sessions unless they want you to fulfil a specific role – in which case they will probably not wait until your job-planning meeting to do so. Clearly this requirement was designed for surgeons et al but in principle one has to go through the ritual dance.

No such stipulation exists for medico-legal work but in both cases your manager has a legitimate interest in knowing something about what you do. There is no requirement for you to tell them how much you earn though many would love to know. A benign explanation of this thirst for knowledge would be that it is a proxy for how much time you spend. Better to tell them how much time you spend then!

A job plan has to be agreed, at the end of the day, so it is really by way of a negotiation, albeit one where the sides are not necessarily equally balanced. You should be looking for what you need, whilst bearing in mind the needs of your employer. Many Trusts are happy for their consultants to do, say, one or two medico-legal reports a week in Trust time, more so if you are a forensic psychiatrist; some private organisations encourage this – then take a cut! You are less likely to be allowed to do private work in Trust time so this, and in many cases medico-legal work too, needs to be done in evening and weekends, unless you can negotiate that your 10 PAs are not worked between Monday and Friday 9-5.

If you want to do your work in your Trust's premises you need to be clear that this is sanctioned by your manager – they may want paying – this is only to be expected but would be a deductible expense for your business. These things have to be discussed – avoidance can lead down the path of your probity being brought into question.

The important thing is to be open about what you do and everyone should be satisfied that you are not spending so much time and attention on this work that you are not able to give adequate attention to your Trust duties. Whilst the negotiation can, at times, be uncomfortable, you will sleep easier afterwards knowing that everything is above board.

Time management

If you are one of those people who is always punctual, can compartmentalise their lives and always manages to fit things

It's a Shrinking Business

in, skip to the next chapter. Everyone else read on! Still with us? – here goes:

If you have never been on a time management course, find one and do it! You may actually learn something If you are going to be doing three things at once (your day job, your personal life and your burgeoning private or medico-legal practice) you had better get used to juggling things. Of course some people are always going to be better at this than others but you can learn and you can improve.

The first thing to do is to create a particular time in the week when you can do this work and arrange things accordingly. This includes any room hire, childcare and support services such as secretarial support. Even if you are not at the stage where you will fill a weekly slot, it is as well that people know when it is, so try not to make yourself too available for other things at this time or it will soon be eroded.

One way of doing this is to use the time for other business related activities until you have people to see. Perhaps speaking to GPs or giving talks on psychiatry, maybe finding out which solicitors in your area need expert reports done.

Delegation

When you start you will have to do almost everything yourself. However very quickly you will realise the benefit of delegation. Unlike in the NHS where things are either given to you or not, in business you will have to buy or pay for them! Typing short letters and reports is fine but sooner or later you will want something more. Whatever you do, don't pay money to people to do things for you without reading the Chapter 7 - on employment - or you may all too easily find yourself breaking the law. In particular please don't fall into the trap of paying your NHS secretary (should you be lucky enough to still have one) to do your private or medico-legal work without understanding your legal responsibilities as an employer.

Clearly this does not mean, either, that you can ask them to work for free – or pass the work off as Trust work – this would clearly raise serious probity issues. Yet I mention it because we have probably all heard of both happening.

However, there are other things you may want to consider – voice transcription technology is continually improving and software is very affordable. It is not for everyone but many colleagues swear by it.

Another aspect to consider is how people contact you. Of course if they ring you at your NHS office you cannot ignore them but you do need to consider the official way in which you should be contacted. If you do your work at a private hospital this may well be sorted, but if you work elsewhere or do medico-legal work you may like to explore other options. Clearly your mobile phone is one – but you do need to be a bit cautious as this could easily intrude into your NHS job and speaking to GPs about private patients (unless in an emergency) or solicitors about clients, during your ward rounds is going to be frowned upon. Answering services – a number of which you can find on the web - are certainly one solution to explore.

In this chapter we have looked at the importance of creating some protected time for you to do your private or medico-legal work. If you work in the NHS you must declare this in your job plan and in order to be effective you need to manage your time well. As things get busier you need to think about delegating activities to prevent work encroaching on personal and NHS time.

Chapter 5 - Your workplace

In this chapter we will look at where you can work from and the legal restrictions which may apply. We will also consider various virtual and non-geographical services which can aid you in setting up a business when you don't have much money to spend.

Location

Whether you are seeing private patients or writing medico-legal reports, the bottom line is that you need somewhere to see the people you are interviewing and this place needs to be clean, warm and present a sufficiently professional aura for people to feel confident in you as a doctor. So it is hardly surprising that many people will consider seeing people in their daytime place of work. As mentioned above this comes with several caveats, the most important of which is getting the permission of the Trust you work for. It is much more common for medico-legal reports where there are few constraints as to where people can be seen.

Although many people work in hospital settings where the Trust will have planning permission to see patients, some

Trust offices do not have such permission and clinical work is done in a different location. Whilst these offices might be acceptable for seeing clients for medico-legal reports they will not be acceptable for seeing patients.

In any case it is unlikely that you will be given permission to see private patients in Trust premises unless special arrangements have been made which are shared between the consultant body. These do exist but are more common in general medical Trusts.

A more common location for seeing private patients is a private hospital. You do not need a psychiatric hospital to see outpatients so you can apply for practising privileges at any hospital. If you are unlucky enough not to have such a hospital and your Trust cannot accommodate you, you might need to look for premises which have D1 planning permission. This category covers health, nursery, religious, museum, art displays and public use. Sometimes developers apply for this to make their offices more attractive. However this is not always an easy option so it will be considered below under the heading of 'Expanding' (Chapter 8) when this usually becomes more of an issue. If you are lucky enough to find such premises, the good news is that even if you only work one session in the NHS, you are currently exempt from registering with the CQC. But beware, rules change – there is more about this in Chapter 8.

Virtual and non-geographic services

If you think about it, businesses need addresses to send things to and these days this must include email. Furthermore having a website is de rigeur these days. People tend to be a little suspicious of you if you don't have a web presence and it is a great opportunity for you to put yourself across to a wider audience. When you do this, be aware that you have to put the name of your business on the website. This is especially important if you are using a trading name as the headline of the website – e.g. Dr J Bloggs trading as SuperShrink (don't call your practice by this name by the way – it implies you are better than others and almost certainly contravenes GMC rules!). There is more about websites in Chapter 8. A phone is quite useful as people do sometimes want to speak to you. So how can you achieve this when you start out? Let's take things one at a time.

A useful way of starting is to get a **PO** (Post Office) Box. This can be literally a place where you collect mail or it can redirect

It's a Shrinking Business

to a geographic address. Costs have gone up recently but it probably beats using your home address up front (although if this is the underlying address it is not secret and people can find out). When you start out you can create stationery on your computer with this address and it can also be used for invoices.

When you register as a 'sole trader' you can trade as any name you like. It could be simply your professional name or you could use some combination of your name and terms such as consultancy, services, practice or the like. It makes sense to link this to an available internet domain name and to purchase this in as many iterations as you think reasonable, e.g. .co.uk, .com, .biz, .info etc. One you will use to promote your business, the others will 'point' there to minimise confusion (and prevent its use) should someone else want to use the same name.

When you start you may just want to have some very basic details on one page; later you may want some more detail. If you can afford it, get a good designer. 'Real businesses' take money to set up; you may have little when you start so you can upgrade as you go along. Either way you can use the forwarding function of any domain name to create a professional email address; enquiries@drbloggs.co.uk rather than joebloggs@virgin.net. If you use this method you will need to ensure outgoing emails come from the same 'alias'. It might also be wise to direct replies there too, as later on you may move this official email to a secretary and this will ensure that 'customers' who just hit 'reply' on an old email in order to reach you get directed to the right person. Alternatively (and frankly much more simply, once set up), for a small fee, you can create this address in its own right based on the domain provider's URL (uniform resource locator).

Next consider getting a computerised phone number. A number of different companies provide these services (see the Webography for an example of such a company). You can get a local number or a non-geographic one which, in the early days can simply be routed to your phone. Later you can direct it to other numbers (e.g. your assistant) or a computerised switchboard. But by having the same number throughout you will not lose custom later on as returning or referred 'customers' lose track of you.

Get a second number with this and it can be used as a 'fax to email' number via the same company. Although fax, per se, is a rapidly aging technology, people (especially solicitors – who are generally quite conservative) still seem to expect it and it saves them having to scan documents at their end. Your phone can automatically be directed to voicemail if you are not available and this will be forwarded to you as an email with a MP3 file attached which you can listen to.

Lastly, if you are doing medico-legal work I strongly recommend getting a DX address if there is a local outlet – often your nearest solicitor will point you in the right direction. DX (Document Exchange) is an alternative postal system much beloved of solicitors because they are not charged by weight and they love sending you bulky packages! Get a DX address and they will not only love you but understand that you mean business!

In this chapter we have covered the issue of finding somewhere to see patients and/or clients. We also discussed the various ways in which you can make yourself available to be contacted with minimal expense in the early days. Having a full range of methods, which are 'portable', causes less loss of custom later on, as you expand.

Chapter 6 - Getting paid

In this chapter we will look at the practicalities of getting paid. If you have no overheads, any money you earn is just 'nice to have'. But we all have one big overhead and it is called tax. In general terms you are taxed on what you charge rather than what you have in the bank (and especially so if what you had in your bank has already been spent!), so you had better be sure you have it before the tax bill comes in, if for no other purpose. Once you start expanding, though, you will have more overheads and sometimes paying the bills seems to be all the business is about. So starting off in a professional way, as you mean to go on, is a good idea and makes for a much more balanced relationship between your professional work as a psychiatrist and your need for money as a business person.

Invoicing

One of the most basic things about any service business, such as we are engaged in, is having a transparent invoicing system. This starts with letting people know the basis on which they will be charged and ends with the invoicing system you use. It does not have to be anything more than a simple word processing programme when you start, though clever accounts packages exist – some quite inexpensive.

This may come as a huge surprise to some of my colleagues, but actually numbering your bills matters! Why? Well, if the taxman decides to audit you they will want to know that you have a system in place to which they can easily relate. If your invoices do not seem to have any rhyme or reason to them and, for example, they see a large gap between July and September (assuming, always, that you actually date them) they may not so easily accept your story that you were away sunning yourself in the Canaries.

On the other hand if invoices are sequentially numbered and you have long fallow periods they can be much more reassured that you know what you are doing and can account clearly for those gaps. You don't have to have any particularly sophisticated system but there must be transparency. Just as you conduct your clinical practice with one eye over your shoulder for the GMC, so it must be with your business practice and HMRC. Keep good records, and if they are electronic make sure they are adequately backed up either electronically or with good, old-fashioned, paper.

Accounts function

Your business needs an 'accounts function'. In the early days it may be you; later it could be a general factotum or a bookkeeper/accounts manager/debt-chaser. But it is important to separate this from clinical or professional matters. Sooner or later you will be faced with a non-paying patient or solicitor and you need to be able to distinguish this from your duty to the patient or the court. There is no room for emotion here. If you decide to start doing this yourself, have a low threshold for delegating it later as it is easy to do it badly and then discover suddenly that you have no money and you are really not of the right temperament (most psychiatrists aren't) to 'chase' people.

Getting money out of people

There are some truths which are eternal. Getting money up front is extremely important. Although getting a credit card machine is associated with some onerous rules and regulations, the company which supplies them can hold your hand as you fill in the wordy yearly questionnaires. But they are really worth their weight in gold (beware, though, you need to have at least some money coming in before you are allowed one!).

It's a Shrinking Business

This is good for (non-insured) private patients – immediately after they have seen you, I would suggest.

Getting money in the bank (good practice dictates that this should be a separate client account) before they are seen (by whatever means) is also advisable for medico-legal self-payers (and we can expect many more of these in the future with legal aid cuts). This is because, once they have seen your report they may feel less inclined to pay. By adopting this approach you not only ensure payment but also distance yourself from any idea that your (independent) report is written favourably in order to please your 'customer'.

Solicitors, as a rule, have no respect for the timescales you might put for payment on your invoices. The sooner you accept this, the better. Years of experience have taught me that the only way to get money out of some of them (of course not all) is to chase them till Kingdom come. Where you are not constrained by the legal aid system, try and build this into your pricing structure. In other words acknowledge that chasing a debt of £100 may, in a certain percentage of cases, cost you an hour of employees' time plus a year's worth of interest at 8% above the base rate (this is the amount that, theoretically at least, you have the right to charge under the

It's a Shrinking Business

Late Payment of Commercial Debts (Interest) Act 1998 and charge slightly more accordingly. At the very least, use this as an aide memoire to review your fees, annually – no-one thanks you for hiking up your fees by enormous amounts after 5 years of stasis.

Of course this is easier said than done but you see where I am going with this. Debt-chasing is a business cost and there is no point tying yourself into knots about it. Some people give discounts for early payment – you may like this idea. Alternatively, like many others, you may accept that early payers subsidise late payers just as cash payers will effectively have to subsidise credit card payers (as it is unusual for professionals to charge extra fees for using credit cards). You have to be willing to set your rates accordingly.

Another idea along the same lines is factoring; businesses exist which will 'buy' your debt for about 75% of its value and pay you 'up front'. Unfortunately this is only applicable to a narrow range of work – classically personal injury reports. But if you do a lot of these for solicitors (as opposed to agencies – who themselves exist on exactly this system – which is why they seem to always be going out of business) it may be worth considering.

It's a Shrinking Business

I have also come across enterprising solicitors who invite you to up your hourly rate by, say 20% in exchange for being paid at the end of the case which might be many years down the line. As long as you do not only do this sort of work, it is something you could consider as 'part of the mix'. But do beware of this sort of work mounting up as you will recall that you have to pay tax on what you charge, not what you have been paid.

Managing the relationship

At the end of the day, putting aside ethics and good professional practice, your patient or solicitor is your customer, and, as such, your bread and butter. Now we all can think of examples of solicitors who are so egregious in their failure to pay that you really do not want an on-going relationship with them. But the vast majority are probably too preoccupied with their professional role and are not that good at running their businesses. They may be good solicitors but bad businessmen. You have to make choices. Chasing is fine but at the end of the day you may have no (sensible) choice but to (at least threaten to) take legal action.

It's a Shrinking Business

The practicalities of this can be found on the Money Claim Online website (see Webography at the end of this book). If you are considering doing this my recommendation is to fill in the form (called an MCOL) and send them a covering letter with a copy giving them 7 days to pay or the MCOL will be issued. Then, if they do not pay, issue it forthwith! 90% of solicitors will pay when faced with a summons – the other 10% are about to go bankrupt in which case you would not be doing business with them in future anyway.

In fact because, in a significant number of cases, imminent bankruptcy is an important reason for solicitors not paying, getting in early with your claim makes total sense as once a solicitor has gone bankrupt getting money out of them can be a complex and longwinded process and you may never see your money. If this happens to you, at least you can 'write it off' as 'bad debt' on your yearly accounts. Sadly all this talk of suing is a reflection of the times – if I had been writing this book 5 years ago it would not have featured so strongly in my thinking. But recessions are a regular part of the world in which we live and several will come around in the lifetimes of most readers. During recessions businesses fail – it is an evolutionary effect – the fittest survive. Solicitors (and doctors) are by no means immune.

It's a Shrinking Business

This happens less frequently with patients – particularly if you 'train' them to pay immediately after being seen, but you have to be much more careful. It is, of course, easier if you have stopped seeing someone; but not, perhaps, if you have reason to believe that they are not well. In these circumstances I suggest you have a very low threshold for contacting your defence organisation before proceeding as the issues to be weighed up are more subtle.

Most patients and many solicitors pay on time but in the middle are all those people who take so many person-hours of chasing. What to do? Well, the answer is, assuming you have taken my advice above, that you just have to live with the tension. You need them and they need you. It's a bit like a dysfunctional marriage really. Sometimes you say enough is enough but most of the time you trudge on together. My experience suggests that it is most often due to inefficiency, particularly common in some smaller solicitors' offices. Sometimes they get a new person in who sorts it out and at other times they overpay you for one bill which you can deduct from the next one (one only wishes this happened more often!).

When you go to courses about getting paid they are always very aggressive about this sort of thing. However, in real life this rarely pays and it is better to be patient and forgiving and to keep their custom and good will – in most cases at least.

In this chapter we have covered the basics of tax compliant invoicing, the importance of building in the costs of debt recovery and the various ways in which late payments can be mitigated or addressed. It was emphasised that having an 'accounts function' separate from your professional or clinical function is a healthy way to approach your work. Finally we discussed the tension between getting paid and maintaining a good relationship with your customers.

It's a Shrinking Business

Chapter 7 - Employing people

In this chapter we will look at the correct way to go about employing people, which you will inevitably have to do if you want to expand your business. As well as the general rules for employment we will consider the types of help you may need and how not to fall foul of employment or equality legislation.

Employment and other laws

It is alarming how many doctors, who are otherwise law-abiding, delude themselves when it comes to employing people. Paying 'cash-in-hand', is almost certainly going to be unlawful in all but the most exceptional of cases (and I am not even going to go there) and we, as doctors, cannot afford to break the law, so here is how to do it:

Firstly, unless the employee is on a prescribed list of close relatives, if you employ anyone you have to have Employers' Liability Insurance. No ifs, no buts; it is laid out clearly in the Employers' Liability (Compulsory Insurance) Act 1969. It can usually be bought cheaply with Public Liability Insurance and is often combined with premises insurance (useful if you have any).

It's a Shrinking Business

Next, it is perfectly acceptable to employ anyone without a formal interview or competitive process (though we shall return to this below). Thus, asking your NHS secretary if s/he would like to work for you – as long as it is out of NHS hours – is fine. I hope you will be paying him or her considerably above the minimum wage (might I suggest something commensurate with what s/he might earn in the NHS?) so I shan't dwell on that bit of legislation other than to mention its existence!

The easiest (and most would argue these days, the only sensible) way to employ people is to utilise the payroll function attached to many accountants' practices. This is because it is fiendishly complicated and hemmed in by all sorts of rules and regulations which seem to change every 5 minutes. They usually charge very reasonable rates and take the headache away from you. When you start they will explain that you need formal contracts as well as disciplinary and grievance procedures to be given to each employee (we will consider what else you need when you get more than 5 employees later).

They can help you design these and you can then duplicate them with alterations for any subsequent employees. You do not have to employ people for any specific time period; theoretically you can have finite contracts. But if your problem is just the scarcity of work in the first few years then zero-hours contracts are a good solution. Work done is effectively 'overtime' but be aware that these workers are entitled to holiday pay based on the average time they have worked in the preceding 3 months.

Once you set things up with payroll, all the other headaches you might have had disappear. So, for example your employee is likely to have a *liability* to pay tax and National Insurance but the *responsibility* to pay it is yours as the employer. Worry not; your friendly payroll department will issue you with a monthly bill to pay to HMRC!

But just before you get your employee to sign the contract, bear in mind the future. Equality and immigration legislation means that you have to treat all potential employees equally, as well as checking that they are entitled to work in the UK. Whilst this may seem nonsensical if it seems evident to you that the person is British, born and bred, trust me that you are better playing by the rules from the off.

So ask your potential employee to bring you their passport. If it is a UK one, photocopy the page with their picture on *in black and white*. Apparently, according to the exact letter of the law (which is often quoted to you if you try and get a copy of your passport in a commercial outlet) making a colour copy may, conceivably, be interpreted as creating a document which could be used as a forgery.

Then file it in their personnel file – which you have (of course) just created and which will later contain their contract, any appraisals and any training they do! If it is not a UK one or they don't have a passport, immediately take advice from your payroll team before signing them up. You will also need to make sure the payroll people get your prospective employee's date of birth, national insurance number and appropriate tax paperwork – either a P45 or a P46 usually. They will let you know though!

Apart from a secretary/general factotum, who might you need to employ? Depending where you are in your business expansion you may need a bookkeeper/accounts person/debt chaser or a receptionist. If you do a lot of reports you may wish to employ someone to proof-read them (I do). Sometimes the same person can do all these tasks, sometimes not. It is important not to force people into roles they do not relish – they rarely do them well!

Advertising and interviewing

You may need to advertise. If so and you have taken part in interviewing in the NHS, you will have some concept as to how to conduct interviews fairly. If not, here are the basic rules:

Start with a written job description and a person specification – it is a good idea to have these anyway even if you do not advertise. You can advertise by any means you see fit. We got a receptionist from a free advert in Tesco's whilst our accounts manager came through an ad in the paper.

Use objective criteria to shortlist – compare people against your person spec and note where they fall short. Keep all documentation! Arrange interviews in a formal and professional manner – ideally have two people interviewing so you can compare notes and have a witness if things go very 'pear-shaped' later. Consider not only speaking to applicants but also giving them tasks. We once interviewed someone who was fine to talk to but when we gave her a simulated phone-answering task, ran out of the door at the mention of the word psychiatrist!

Don't be rushed into a decision but make it on the basis of objective criteria – still keeping all the paperwork. If you have asked for references, the job offer should be made conditionally, subject to these being satisfactory.

Managing your employee(s)

Your responsibilities do not stop once you have employed someone. Though perhaps in a less bureaucratic way, many of the things which you are familiar with from the NHS workplace still need to occur for your employees. At some level you need to have some form of risk assessment process which enables you to decide whether further checks are required.

In the absence of any requirement for patient/client contact (e.g. a typist who works at home) you may decide that a DBS (Disclosure and Barring Service - previous known as CRB - Criminal Records Bureau) check is not necessary but otherwise, I suggest you may be well-advised to have one. You may ask for forms from elsewhere but, if necessary, there are companies which can assist you to do your own checks (See Webography). If you sign up with one of these companies you will have to have your own ex-offender policy. As with any other policy you can research what others do on the internet. Even were it not a requirement it is a good idea to have one and to combine it with a risk assessment, which you have thought through, suitable for your practice. What will you do if, when you do an enhanced DBS check – necessary for working with children and vulnerable adults, you find that a prospective employee has a 'spent' conviction for theft? Your response has to be proportionate, remember.

Appraisals are a good idea – you sometimes find out some interesting things and they demonstrate that you are taking an ongoing interest in your employees' welfare. You can use forms from elsewhere (subject to any copyright issues) or design your own. Safeguarding children and vulnerable adult training is something you should consider for all staff in contact with patients or clients. Certainly these sorts of things will feature should you ever be regulated by the CQC. Appraisals do not have to be onerous but you should allocate an hour or so a year to sit down and review things. Always allow your employees to give their views. You may find something out!

It's a Shrinking Business

Before too long legislation will require you to contribute to your employees' pensions; your payroll department will advise you when this starts to apply to small businesses but you could choose to do this already if you wish to and your payroll department can advise you about tax efficient ways of doing this, for example through 'salary sacrifice'.

Lastly you may need to dismiss someone – for example if your business contracts or you want to retire. Always seek guidance if there are contentious issues. The notice period will be part of their contract and may be longer for people who have been there some while. Always consider very carefully and, where possible, agree this on an amicable basis. But do not delay making a decision. Businesses naturally expand and contract and if you do not contract accordingly if your revenue decreases, you may find yourself in the same unfortunate position as that solicitor you were suing in Chapter 6!

If your circumstances change and you do not need to employ a person in a particular function anymore it may be that you can make them redundant. Again you should take advice (e.g. from your payroll department or a Citizens Advice Bureau) if someone has been with you for longer than 2 years, as statutory redundancy pay may need to be paid and there has to be a proper consultation beforehand with written notification.

A similar thing would apply in the unfortunate event that you had to dismiss someone for failing to do their job adequately where informal and/or formal warnings might be required; you will need to be guided as to the correct actions to take along the way (e.g. from your payroll department, a Citizens Advice Bureau or even an employment lawyer). Thankfully this is not a common occurrence.

In this chapter we have covered the basic law applying to employing people as well as the practicalities of getting the 'correct' employee in place and, if necessary dismissing them. We have also looked at the training and support which you need to provide for your employees whilst they are with you.

It's a Shrinking Business

Chapter 8 - Expanding

In this chapter we will look at how you get from being someone who does the odd report or sees the odd private patient to someone who has a thriving and hopefully growing practice. Obviously the degree to which you aspire to this depends on what stage of your career you are at, but the principles remain similar. We will also consider what extra laws and regulations come into play as you grow.

How to get more work

There is little doubt that the best way to get more work is by recommendation. Hence, being good at what you do is not only good ethically and clinically but also, possibly, your strongest business tool. And being good encompasses the classic 'As' of private and medico-legal practice: ability, affability and availability. To which I might add administration (which may be delegated).

Hopefully you are already able and will get more so by continually reviewing your CPD needs and training for your expanding role. Hopefully you can be pleasant to patients, colleagues and solicitors (or, in the latter case, find someone to act as your 'front' who can be) so let us think a bit more about availability. In medico-legal work solicitors sometimes find they need an expert to confirm their availability during a court case; if you have a system which enables you or your assistant to answer the phone then and there you are more likely to be instructed. In private practice, if you can promise an appointment that week, you are more likely to get GPs referring to you and patients recommending you. A lot of this is about two things: appropriate delegation and time management.

Another way in which to get more work is by 'putting yourself about'. Networking, giving talks to GPs and lawyers, being available for free informal advice, writing articles for 'trade journals' and giving lectures are all examples. If you do medico-legal work it may be worth being in one or two expert witness directories, so people can find you if they have incomplete details. However, make sure you have a system for monitoring what brings people to you, so you can work out if these are really of any use. My experience suggests they are probably not terribly helpful in the bigger scheme of things and can cost quite a lot of money year on year (though this is always tax deductible!).

Remember that the GMC rules allow you to promote yourself in an equitable and ethical manner. They do not allow you to make claims that you are somehow unique or better than other colleagues. Make sure you understand your professional boundaries in this regard before you put together any promotional material.

Make sure you website is kept up to date and 'drives' people towards contacting you. Search engine optimisation is all the rage. Get a blog on your website so the words change regularly. Use social media both to contact colleagues and to 'push' them towards your website and your business. To make all this happen my advice is to find yourself a good designer *not*, primarily, a web/technical person – the latter, in my experience, is putting the cart before the horse. Once you have a good design, all the technical stuff should follow (good designers will work with 'techies'). This includes the 'statutory stuff' like making sure there is a notice about cookies, as well as the important practical stuff like making sure the website is adapted for smart phones and is easily changeable by yourself in the future.

Lastly, if you find yourself getting busier - do something about it. If your waiting lists simply get longer and longer you will be in danger of losing your 'edge' and people may stop instructing or referring to you. At this point you have three constructive choices:

1. Change your work pattern, e.g. drop **NHS** sessions, though this is not only easier said than done but hard to reverse if things go 'pear-shaped' in your business.

2. Take on 'help' either in the form of staff, if relevant, or colleagues. The colleagues could be psychologists, psychiatrists of other disciplines or just another person who does whatever you do.

3. Make arrangements to send work elsewhere (if you really don't want to do anymore).

Legal aspects of expanding

As you start to employ more people you will find that your administration gets more complex and there is a need for more policies and procedures. For example if you have more than 5 employees you may need to have access to a stakeholder pension for them. Before too long you will need to pay all your employees pensions contributions. Similarly you may need to have a driving policy (even if no-one has to drive for work). Your payroll provider, an IFA or your accountant (because by now you will certainly need one!) can usually advise you about these matters.

You should have child and vulnerable adult safeguarding policies. If you cease doing NHS work and practise privately you will need to be regulated by the CQC and they will certainly require you to have them. In this regard, as already mentioned, take care to check the up to date situation as generally regulation increases over time. Check the CQC website with regard to the requirements of both individuals and practices to register with the CQC. Data protection/information security and risk assessment/health and safety policies are also things you should have.

If you do medico-legal work and your income crosses the VAT (value added tax) threshold (see the HMRC website for up to date information on what this threshold is) you will need to register for VAT and charge it on all qualifying bills. Your accountant can advise you further but this may be the point at which you feel the need to delegate more of your accounts function as doing quarterly returns for VAT can be time consuming.

Professional consequences of ceasing work in the NHS

In order to continue to practise as a doctor, you need regular appraisals and revalidation. At the point that you sever your links with the NHS, unless you work for another managed organisation you will have to make your own arrangements. If you only do medico-legal work, whilst the GMC does not require you to have a licence to practise, the medical defence organisations have said that they do and probably by the time you read this all the courts, tribunals and professional panels who instruct you will also (effectively or actually) require it. This means that, if you are not aligned with a private hospital, you will have to make a decision about how you get your appraisals and who your responsible officer (RO) will be.

You have several choices. The Independent Doctors Federation (IDF) is for doctors of all hues and your appraiser may or may not be a psychiatrist, the Medical Support Union (MEDSU) is a co-operative organisation set up for psychiatrists and the Doctors Appraisal Consultancy can help with advice on both appraisal and revalidation. In addition, the GMC has a system of 'Suitable Persons' which may be worth exploring depending on your circumstances (see Webography for all of these).

Teaming up

Working on your own, with maybe one or two employees can be fun but can also be difficult. If you are considering increasing the amount of work you do there are a number of different models of working you could consider, The first is to work with others in a loose structure. This makes sense if you want to increase the range of services you offer. For example, if you are an adult psychiatrist and are referred a child, instead of turning away the referral you can simply say that this is the province of your colleague Dr X and make arrangements (with the consent of all parties) for the patient or client to be seen by this colleague.

The referrer does not need to know your business relationship with Dr X, who might simply be a colleague practising separately at a different address. Alternatively, especially if you have premises, you might want to rent Dr X a room or charge a fixed fee or a percentage of the fee they charge the patient (not to mention Dr Y the older age psychiatrist). Both these models are forms of association and do not constitute a legal entity. It is important that any associate is free to work for others or independently so as not to create a situation of de facto employment. Employing doctors or therapists is not generally a useful way forward in the early stages, fraught as it is with the sort of responsibility which requires you to insure or indemnify yourself vicariously on their behalf. Mutual benefit is the name of the game.

If you have one or more colleague(s) who want to take business risks with you, or a spouse/partner who earns little or no money elsewhere, you may consider forming some sort of partnership, either a simple one or a limited liability one (LLP). The pros and cons depend on your circumstances and are outside the scope of this book but you should *always take advice*, initially from your accountant but probably also from a solicitor.

Some doctors form companies. There are different types, such as the traditional limited company (Ltd) or a community interest company (CIC); again, *these decisions require careful advice*. A key issue is the different taxation structure of a company, but this does not suit everybody's circumstances. These structures all have their pros and cons. The obvious downside with a company is that whilst its profits are taxed at a lower rate, as soon as you take money out (to spend) you will be taxed at your normal rate. Perhaps this type of structure might suit someone who does not need money now but would like it later when they are not earning so much from other employment. But *never take advice about such matters from the author of a 'self-help' book!* Consult a professional, because at different times and for different circumstances the advice will almost certainly differ.

In this chapter we have covered some of the ways in which you can increase your practice, particularly the importance of personal recommendations. We have discussed some of the legal and regulatory requirements you have to comply with, particularly if you have left the NHS entirely. Lastly we looked at some of the various legal entities which you can use to team up with people.

It's a Shrinking Business

Chapter 9 - Succession planning

Nothing lasts forever – and this includes your career. Put better, it makes sense to think of your working life as consisting of different stages. Furthermore, people have different philosophies and ideas about what makes for a pleasant life. Some want to give up work altogether at a single point in time – retirement pure and simple. Many others will be reading this book because they have nominally retired from the NHS but wish to pursue other avenues. But none of us can go on forever and it is a matter of probity that we should think ahead and not leave our patients or 'customers' in the lurch. Although it may be painful to think about it, winding down in one shape or form is necessary for us all - failure to plan ahead may lead to an abrupt or messy end to a career - which is not desirable.

At the professional level this consists of deciding what you will *not* be doing next month and/or next year. If you are doing medico-legal work you may decide, at relatively short notice, not to take on new work. From a professional viewpoint this is fine but, as we shall see below, from a business point of view there are better ways of handling this. However there are always addenda reports, court appearances and follow-up reports to be considered so it is important to plan ahead so that if you do 'pull the plug' and become non-contactable, it will not be at a time when you are most likely to be needed.

Similarly with private patients; you may wish to slowly wind down, discharging people and not taking on any new referrals, but there may well be some people whom you think should receive ongoing care – albeit not from yourself.

However, the big issue is not a professional one but a business one. What doctors often do not realise is that what they do may have value to others. Realistically psychiatric practices are not going to be bought up by hedge funds but a medical practice, which by all accounts can take eight years to build up, may well have value to other doctors. However, even before we talk about this it may be worth your while *taking advice* on whether, within the time you are still working you sell your own business to a company. And by this I mean a company owned by yourself (maybe with others). This is because if there is value in the business, there may be tax benefits in so doing. And these tax benefits are likely to maximised if the value of the business is enhanced by the income brought in by others.

Which is why succession planning starts early. Knowing what I just told you, you may decide that there is value to be had in working with colleagues. If, over ten years you have earned x and your colleagues have earned y, the value of the business if sold to a company (yours or someone else's) may be a multiple of y. Whilst it may well include an element of x, it is likely to be y which matters more. But please, I reiterate, *don't take my word for it*. If this book prompts you to book an appointment with your accountant this will be no bad thing.

Whether or not you decide to adopt the model of working with others for this reason, you may well decide to hand over some or part of your practice anyway. Whilst these may well start as professionals reasons - patients who need continuing support and care - if you think far enough ahead and can find someone who understands the commercial benefits of a 'going concern' there may well be several different ways to get value out of your years of hard-earned effort.

At the simplest level, if your (probably younger) colleague were to start up a practice tomorrow s/he might earn a small amount, but by working with you (who by now will have a more impressive yearly income) s/he will ally her or himself with a 'brand' which has perceived ongoing value. One way of 'monetising' this if you think far enough ahead is to give your practice a name which can outlive your time in it. Dr Jones' Practice sounds fine for when Dr Jones is around but people might be disappointed to hear that they will be seen by Dr Smith. However, if you give your practice a neutral name or add the word 'Associates' you keep your options open. Furthermore, if it is always understood by the outside world that the practice has more than one practitioner, when you eventually decide to step aside or reduce your workload, the work can go on with nary a hiccup.

This is worth money in anyone's book and all that remains is to find some way to make it pay. This is the bit where you need to take some advice from at least an accountant and maybe a solicitor but anything which has value must have a price and thus all that remains is to find the correct legal vehicle for realising this. And there are various ways of doing this. One general way, which may be attractive to both the outgoing and the incoming principal, is to have some sort of arrangement whereby the person who will be retiring in the future hands over the reins slowly. This provides stability for the business, reassurance for the incoming principal and comfort (and money) for the outgoing one. Of course any business situation where everyone is happy is all to the good.

If all this seems obvious to you it is possibly because you have direct or indirect experience of some other industry or profession. Or have worked in another country. Or are familiar with the way NHS general practice works in the UK. The concept of specialist doctors selling an interest in their business or selling a company as an ongoing concern is relatively rare in the UK, yet as we move further away from the nationalised industry model of the NHS it is inevitable that this will become more commonplace. The classic model of selling a company would be based on a multiple of yearly income generated other than by the labour of the retiring principal. This money could be paid back over an agreed timeframe from the ongoing profits of the business and quite often part of the deal is for the retiring principal to stay on for an agreed time as a director to keep a steadying hand on the tiller. Meaning that waiting until the last minute before ceasing work is not really a very good idea!

In this chapter we have considered the ethical issues with approaching the end of your working life, thought about the value of the business you have built up and talked about the different ways in which you might hand over the work and gain value from doing this. Lastly, as with any major decision, *don't rely on a self-help book.* Take appropriate professional advice!

Chapter 10 - Putting it into practice

I hope you have enjoyed reading the book, so far. Unless you are already quite experienced, you have probably had to absorb quite a lot of new concepts and, from my experience of speaking to colleagues, I know that old habits and beliefs are sometimes quite difficult to shift and new concepts hard to assimilate. So in this chapter I am going to ask you to do a bit of work. If you are lazy you can just go on to the answers, but give it a go if you are up for the challenge. Here is a 'real life scenario' which, in my experience, is often the way in which people 'get into' private practice:

> Dr Broadbent is a consultant adult psychiatrist who has been in post in an NHS Trust for 2 years. He quite likes the idea of doing a bit of private practice and happens to mention this to one of his catchment area GPs at a social function. The GP says he thinks he might have one or two patients he would be happy to refer. Two weeks later Dr Broadbent is pleasantly surprised to find a private referral for a lady, Mrs Threpston, which has been sent to Sarah, his NHS secretary.

> Dr Broadbent asks her to set up an appointment where he does his outpatient clinics. He suggests this should be at his office, as opposed to at the local hospital. Sarah rings Mrs Threpston and gives her the details on the phone. She creates a slot in her filing cabinet marked 'Private Patients' and puts the referral letter in there. After he has seen the patient Dr Broadbent dictates a letter to the GP at the end of a number of others and sends the (unencrypted) digital file to Sarah via e-mail. Sarah writes the letter on the ordinary headed paper she uses. It is rather long and takes her 2 hours. She pops it into the post with all the others. Dr Broadbent also asks Sarah to request payment from Mrs Threpston, so she writes a note on plain paper asking her to please send a cheque made payable to Dr Broadbent and post it to his Trust office address. Dr Broadbent thanks Sarah and gives her a ten pound note for doing the typing.

What I would invite you to do, is to think about the above scenario and make a note of anything you feel Dr Broadbent has done incorrectly.

Has he broken any laws? Are there things he could have done better? When you have finished, check below to see how well you did:

What Dr Broadbent should have done

The version below describes a 'parallel universe' where Dr Broadbent does all the correct things:

As soon as he mentions to the GP that he would like to do some private practice, Dr Broadbent realises that he needs to do something about this. He tells the GP that he will look into setting things up and will tell him if and when he is ready but asks him not to refer anyone beforehand.

He contacts Dr Anwar, his medical director and tells him he would like a review of his job plan because he would like to do some private practice. They arrange a meeting for the next week. Meanwhile he rings his defence organisation and informs them that he wants to work privately. He establishes the threshold above which he needs to pay a higher premium and agrees to let them know when this is crossed.

Dr Broadbent then goes online and registers as a data controller with the Information Commissioner's Office. He follows this up by ringing a local accountant, Mr Muir, and sets up a meeting for the next day. At this meeting, he discusses his plans with the accountant who agrees to act for him and offers the services of his payroll department. They agree that, at this stage, Dr Broadbent will be a sole trader and his accounting year will begin the next month. Mr Muir registers Dr Broadbent as self-employed with HMRC. The day after, he meets the payroll manager who works with his accountant who helps him design a contract for a zero-hours worker and a disciplinary and grievance procedure.

On Saturday, he pops into a local bank and sets up 3 business accounts, current, savings and client. As he is a sole trader, the name on the account will be 'Dr G Broadbent T/A (trading as) Dr G Broadbent Psychiatric Practice'.

Dr Broadbent meets with Dr Anwar and explains his thoughts; he formally offers the Trust a session, which Dr Anwar graciously turns down. They then discuss where he might see patients. Dr Anwar mentions that the local general hospital, which was built in the same grounds as the psychiatric hospital where they both work, has a private suite which rents rooms to consultants. They agree that this is an acceptable location and Dr Anwar says that as far as he is concerned if it is just the occasional referral he is quite happy for Dr Broadbent to see patients there at the beginning or end of the day, even within hours, as long as it does not interfere with his NHS work. They agree to review the job plan if the number of referrals increases to the extent that it is starting to look as if he might need a whole session. Dr Broadbent rings the suite and puts in motion the necessary paperwork to rent rooms there.

Dr Broadbent speak to Sarah to see if she might like to type his private letters and do a bit of admin for him; she agrees, so he explains she would need to do this at home which is fine with her as she has a computer. He checks with her that her computer is password protected and explains that (written or digital) patient data needs to be kept separately in password protected files. They agree the password verbally between them.

Then he orders a foot-pedal for Sarah's computer (so she can type out digital files) and a digital dictaphone for himself (making a mental note to keep the invoices for tax purposes). He asks Sarah to bring in her passport which he takes home overnight to make a black and white photocopy. He puts the copy in a file, which he locks in a cupboard in his dining room which he has set aside for his private practice papers and files. He gives Sarah's national insurance number and date of birth to his accountant's payroll department. In turn they give him a P46 for Sarah to fill in (because she is still employed by the NHS).

Sarah actually has a New Zealand passport, so Dr Broadbent contacts the payroll department to check what he needs to be looking for in terms of her work status. Unsurprisingly (since she is already working for the NHS, who should have checked this out) they are able to reassure him that she is fine to work based on the work visa in her passport, which they ask him to photocopy as well. He, therefore, emails her copies of the contract to sign, together with a useful Excel file which the payroll manager has sent him, enabling Sarah to work out any future holiday pay. The contract stipulates a zero hour contract with a rate well above the adult minimum wage which Sarah is happy with so she signs the contract and returns one copy to Dr Broadbent.

The payroll manager sets Sarah up on their system, which means that they will send Dr Broadbent a payslip for her when he provides them with information about the number of hours she works each month. Dr Broadbent takes a note of Sarah's bank account details to enable him to pay her.

Dr Broadbent then goes online and downloads and fills in in an application for a PO Box based on his home address. He finds a computerised telephony company and hires two lines. One he directs to his own mobile and the other to a fax which redirects to his email. He then seeks out domain names and purchases dr-broadbent-psych.com and .co.uk. He directs enquiries@dr-broadbent-psych.com to his home email address (but makes sure that the replies go to enquiries@dr-broadbent-psych.com in case he later moves email over to a secretary) and makes a note to send outgoing emails from the same 'alias'. He directs the fax line to this email address as well. He then purchases employers liability and public liability insurance (because no insurer sold employer's liability insurance on its own). He makes sure he keeps all the invoices.

That weekend Dr Broadbent wraps a cold towel around his head and devotes his time to creating a beautiful business plan. On Monday morning, he contacts the GP and tells him he is now set up to see private patients and gives him his contact details. Two weeks later Dr Broadbent finds a referral for a Mrs Threpston in his post at home (redirected automatically from the PO Box) and emails Sarah asking her to set up an appointment at the private suite. He tells her to do this on computer-generated headed paper showing his contact details which he has created on his own computer. He also mentions that invoices will be on the same paper but must show the accounting year followed by sequential numbering.

He asks Sarah to send an appointment letter to Mrs Threpston on a template he has designed. This template gives the patient details of his charges, explains that they must be settled by cheque or cash immediately after the appointment, and mentions Dr Broadbent's responsibilities as a data controller and how her data will be used for the purposes of sending appointments and writing letters to her GP (with her consent). Dr Broadbent then goes online and buys himself a digital recorder, a pedal and earphones for Sarah's computer and some files, stamps and envelopes (remembering to keep the receipts). Next he creates a shared facility for his practice work on Google Drive. He establishes that Sarah already uses Google, so has an email address which she accesses it under. He then adds this email address to the list of people who can access the practice work facility. He explains to Sarah how this works and makes sure she can access the drive. He also tells her how to download free software for the pedal (which he has researched online). He then scans his signature for her, asking her to keep it securely on her password-protected computer at home in a password protected file and gives her the stationery he purchased.

All goes ahead as planned and he sees the patient at the private suite, establishes that she is happy for him to write to her GP and that she would like a copy of her GP's letter. After the appointment Mrs Threpston gives him a cheque (made payable to Dr G Broadbent Psychiatric Practice) and he tells her that Sarah will issue an official 'paid' invoice. He then dictates a letter for Sarah; he uploads this to Google Drive (as a MP3 file) and emails Sarah at home to tell her it is there. Sarah accesses the drive, listens to the file, types the letter and uploads it to Google Drive as a Google document (Google documents can be edited on line and are quite useful for clinic letters – reports with a lot of formatting sometimes suffer in the conversion process so uploading [and downloading again to edit] as Word documents may be a better option). She emails Dr Broadbent to tell him it is there. He accesses the file, deletes the MP3 file, edits the letter and tells Sarah by email that it is ready to go. She pastes in his scanned signature (having loaded the software when prompted by Google) and sends the letter to the GP and a copy to the patient by post in the envelopes Dr Broadbent gave her, with a copy to Mrs Threpston, marked confidential.

At the end of the month, Sarah lets Dr Broadbent know how many hours she has worked (including any administration) and he informs the payroll manager. The payroll manager sends Dr Broadbent a note of how much tax he needs to pay HMRC the next month (as you go along this will usually be sent out a month in advance so you can be prepared) and a payslip for Sarah. He passes it on to Sarah, keeping a note of sufficient detail to allow him to set up a payment from his business bank account, which he organises for the end of the month.

Well; take a breath, this was a counsel of perfection and (even assuming I remembered everything and got everything right) very few people would get it right first time (and that includes me). Some of us found things out by trial and error over many years, but you have bought this book so deserve to be told all I have gleaned over the years. You will doubtless have realised that some things are more important than others and ideally you would not want to wait for the pressure of an actual referral being in the offing – but life often works like this. So if you missed things out when you did the exercise, does it matter?

It's a Shrinking Business

What Dr Broadbent did wrong (and was therefore responsible for Sarah doing wrong)

Well the answer is never going to be 100% black and white but here is what I think was wrong with the original scenario:

- Whilst receiving a private referral letter at an NHS address is not a problem per se, Dr Broadbent should have set things up clearly from the start
- Dr Broadbent should not ask an NHS employee to do non-NHS work, during NHS hours
- By setting up the appointment without discussing private practice in his job plan, Dr Broadbent is potentially in breach of his own contract which requires him to offer one session of extra work to the Trust before doing any private practice
- By asking Sarah to set up a private appointment Dr Broadbent is arguably already employing Sarah. Certainly this relationship has been well established by the time he gives her the ten pound note. He has therefore:

    - Failed to check her immigration status (and treat her equitably)

- Failed to provide her with a contract
- Failed to provide her with a disciplinary and grievance procedure
- Failed to be insured as her employer
- Failed to take *responsibility* for paying any tax she owes on her pay
- Failed to establish that he was paying her at or above the minimum wage – including establishing what age bracket she falls into for this purpose. The minimum wage changes year on year but is certainly north of £6 an hour for someone over 21 and over £5 an hour for someone between 18 and 20 (in practice it was below as Sarah is 23 and it took her two hours, you will recall)
- Failed to ensure that in future she can claim holiday pay

- It is quite possible that Dr Broadbent's office, as opposed to the local hospital where he does his outpatient clinics, does not have the D1 planning consent required to see patients so he is potentially breaching local planning law

- Sarah, in ringing Mrs Threpston, is using NHS resources and also doing private work during NHS time
- By creating a slot in her filing cabinet for 'Private Patients' not only is Sarah using NHS resources and doing private work during NHS time, but Dr Broadbent is controlling data without being registered with the Information Commissioner's Office.
- We presume that Dr Broadbent is dictating his letter on NHS equipment
- By sending an unencrypted digital file to Sarah he is arguably not taking sufficient care as a data controller (registered or not). One hopes this is not the normal practice in his Trust as they would presumably be the data controller there, but everyone has a responsibility for abiding by the principles of the Data Protection Act 1998
- Sarah, by writing the letter on ordinary headed paper and posting it via the Trust's system is using NHS resources for private work. All these examples could reasonably engage the attention of NHS Protect (a branch of the NHS Business Agency)
- By asking Sarah to request payment from Mrs Threpston after the event Dr Broadbent has missed a

vital opportunity to get payment from her at the time of her appointment
- A note on plain paper might conceivably be an invoice but it is not part of a proper system, and HMRC would struggle to understand where it fitted into a broader business pattern
- By asking Mrs Threpston to send a cheque to the Trust address, Dr Broadbent is, once again, utilising NHS resources for his own private practice. Additionally there is a clear boundary issue between his business and NHS work.

Well, I hope you spotted all or most of these errors and now feel more confident in your ability to set up and run a legal, ethical and profitable psychiatric business!

Acknowledgements

I would like everyone who has contributed to the genesis of this book. Those who shall not be named include all those people whom I have observed doing things the wrong way; this was the grit in the oyster upon all which came later was founded. After putting on several of my own workshops I was invited to give talks at the Royal College of Psychiatrists and then to give workshops there also. My colleague Andy Macaulay then recommended me to write a CPD module for the Royal College of Psychiatrists and this was the final inspiration for this book.

It's a Shrinking Business

We Need It By Next Thursday – The Joys of Writing Psychiatric Reports

By Danny Allen

If you have enjoyed this book, and have not already read it, here is a sneak preview of We Need It By Next Thursday:

Introduction

In the quarter of a century or so that I have been a psychiatrist, I have noticed that writing medical reports is a bit of a 'Marmite' subject (for those non-Brits amongst you, Marmite is a smelly brown substance which some of us like spreading on our toast – you either love it or you hate it). I have seen people who would rather attend long, boring committee meetings than write a short report for the court on one of their patients, and I have seen others who have written highly inadequate reports and not received any payment for them – probably because they recognised at some level that these reports were not worth paying for. I have been writing reports now for over 20 years and, like so many other people, was introduced to them in earnest by doing a forensic psychiatry job. This certainly gave me good training for writing criminal reports, but did not really prepare me for the huge and exciting field of expert witness work which I later discovered existed out there.

Over the years I have been to numerous courses and done huge amounts of training just to ensure that I am appropriately trained and prepared as an expert witness, but there are still surprises and the working environment is still changing, meaning that the work remains as fresh and exciting as it ever was. I don't know why this is; call me an old softy but there is something about this work which calls me back again and again. Although on the surface there are huge similarities between cases, the differences and the human interest just makes me want to come back for more!

From speaking to my trainees over the years, many like the idea of doing medico-legal reports, but have not been given the opportunity to try, whilst others quite clearly, genuinely do not wish to do this. Of course, I have no problem with those who do not wish to do such work, except to point out that from time to time they may be put under quite a considerable amount of pressure to do so, as part of their day-to-day jobs. Therefore it seems like quite a good idea to know how to do it and to be able to avoid some of the pitfalls associated with being an occasional report writer. Indeed the new ways of assessing trainees means that more do get the opportunity and I feel this is an advance. Since training and mentoring junior doctors is something I enjoy as well it has always been a special treat for me when a trainee not only manages to write a good report but gets the appetite for doing so for its own sake.

Many books have been written about medico-legal report writing, some of which I have found extremely useful and I have listed some of these in the bibliography. However, most of these are written from the head and not the heart. I make no bones about the fact that book is based on emotion. It is an account of why I love doing what I do, written in the hope that some of my readers may go on to love doing what they do. In exactly the same way as I love bread and cheese, but prefer cheese sandwiches, so I enjoy clinical work in parallel with my medico-legal work.

One of the joys of doing medicine in the seventies and eighties was the ability to chop and change specialties, almost at whim. I did not enter psychiatry until I had gone through quite a few different medical careers, including orthopaedics, ENT and General Practice, and I have absolutely no regrets about the fact that I did this. What attracted me to psychiatry when I first did it was the huge range of different sub-specialties within it, and so it is with medico-legal work. Looking back now I can see that the reports I did for the criminal courts form only a small proportion of the sorts of work available. In other words, there is probably something for everyone, and for some of us it is the very variety of work which inspires us

In this little book I hope to give you a flavour of what you might expect doing this sort of work, some of the pitfalls and some of the pleasures. Please do not read it expecting some erudite account of the legal and court system – I leave this for my elders and betters. This is a book about the joys of medical report writing. Enjoy!

Chapter 1 – Do I Need the Aggravation?

It's a Shrinking Business

When I was a senior registrar and started doing medico-legal reports in earnest, I asked one my consultants in general psychiatry who used to do a few reports how he started; he answered straight away, "Buying new shoes for kids is expensive."

Working in the NHS it has become embarrassing for some doctors to talk about money, but if you and I, dear reader, are to be honest with each other, we do rather like being paid well for doing our jobs. And why ever not? Across the world, most doctors charge for their services and there is nothing to be ashamed of in this. There are perfectly ethical ways of doing this and were it not for the motivation to make money businesses, and indeed capitalist societies, would collapse. So if your primary motivation is to make money, do not be ashamed. As I say to my children, "The purpose of education is to allow society to pay you for doing something which you enjoy doing." As professionals, I hope that we enjoy doing our clinical work; I certainly do, and when I worked in the NHS I got paid well for it. In exactly the same way, we should expect to be paid in accordance with our skills if we decide to do medico-legal work.

So that answers your first unspoken question. If we need (or desire) the money we need to do the work to earn it (unless you wish to end up as the subject of a criminal report, of course!). But this does not mean for a minute that this has to be your only motivation because there are lots of other satisfactions to be had in this line of work. For starters, from a public policy point of view, the court system would collapse without experts of one sort or another so we must be performing some sort of useful function even if, from time to time, politicians rail against the expense of paying for our views. Think about this for a moment. Clinical work is important, sure, but how would you feel if, for example, your schizophrenic patient were to be incarcerated for a year for attempting to erect a cross in the middle of the M1. "Can't you see; you would say, this

It's a Shrinking Business

man is obviously unwell and needs treatment". Aha – so you obviously feel impelled to explain to the court the sorts of things which people do when they are deluded and you feel that you could help this man better by admitting him to your ward for 3 weeks. Someone has to explain this to the judge… Why not you? You are, after all, an expert in mental disorder with the ability to communicate and write letters to GPs at least. So how much more difficult can it be to write a court report? And of course, the answer is "Not that much more difficult – but there are a couple of things you need to be aware of…"

And, it is this last bit, quite frankly, which worries (or aggravates) some people. For the occasional report writer, the fear that they might not be aware of some rule or another is enough to put them off the whole thing. But not you my friend! Unless I gave it to you (!) you have probably bought this book because you are flirting with the idea of becoming a medico-legal report writer. To which I say: "Flirt no longer – commit!" Anything worth doing requires some effort and if you wanted a life without aggravation why did you become a doctor? And as a doctor is being a psychiatrist so easy? The key to doing this work is to understand that it is not just an offshoot of clinical psychiatry to be done at a whim but a sort of subspecialty in its own right. Would you become a neuro-psychiatrist without further training? Need I say more?

So; enough talk of aggravation. If you have read this far you probably want to know why it is so much fun; right? Okay, so let's be honest with each other. This is not the same sort of pleasure you get from white-water rafting – okay – it is a little more cerebral than that but then many people would ask you what pleasures you get from conducting a ward round or working within a multi-disciplinary team. What can I tell you? Here is my confession: I get pleasure from the luxury of being able to go through a very full case file, taking notes and forming a hypothesis. The amount of information you get in medico-legal cases is usually much more complete when you see a new patient in out-patients, and you should have (or insist on having) a full copy of the GP notes which can provide lots of rich material.

The next enjoyable part of the process is seeing the client (not a patient – you are not treating them – remember to explain this). However, like a clinical interview, this gives you the opportunity of getting to know a fellow human being, which at the end of the day is what we psychiatrist surely love doing best of all. Although your main job is clearly to write a report

It's a Shrinking Business

I always point out to my trainees that there is often a distinct secondary agenda and this makes for much satisfaction. Nowhere is this more evident than in personal injury cases. The classic case is PTSD; I regularly see people who have soldiered on for two or three years in some considerable distress which they keep thinking will get better – but never does. Make a diagnosis of PTSD, explain that this is an injury and not a mental illness and send them of for treatment by a clinical psychologist and you feel you have done a good day's work. See them 6 months later once treated and you know you are in the right job!

I do a lot of work for the family courts and most of my clients have substance or alcohol abuse problems. Each has a harrowing – but different- story to tell and many of them are hopelessly lacking in insight. However, a small, but significant, proportion has started to 'see the light' and in an even smaller percentage of case, the medico-legal interview can tip them from pre-contemplation to contemplation and sometimes even into real life-changing action. Again I have to tell you that I derive huge pleasure from seeing people for a second time who having listened to what I had to say or who had read and digested my report have taken it upon themselves to do something deep and meaningful to change their lives. These people come back, sit down and talk freely and openly about how they were, what they have discovered about themselves and how they have changed. And very often these are the people who get their kids back in the subsequent court case.

My very last example is of employment cases; these can take a lot of time going through the minutiae of what happened in the workplace and relating this to changes in mental state. But the rewards here too are great. Demonstrating to the client that it was the workplace events which caused their condition can be incredibly validating for them even if you cannot help them do anything about it. But it is also an exercise in very carefully piecing together the evidence which can be very satisfying to those of a slightly obsessional bent.

Whilst I have to confess that my least favourite part of medico-legal work is the actual dictation of the report, the editing of the report in almost every case is a fun pursuit and carefully crafting the conclusions can be very satisfying. I have noticed that some trainees take to this with alacrity whilst others struggle. It is interesting that if you read clinical notes the diagnosis is often vague, or differential, sometimes often crystallising (in often confusing and variable ways) at the point the junior doctor has to put something on the discharge summary. No such vagueness is possible with the medico-legal report and for me this is part of the excitement. The conclusion of any report is your big opportunity to shine. Here you carefully gather in the information you have gleaned, decide whether others may hold a different view, focus in on the questions asked of you (or which you assume the court wants answers to) and then and there, in black and white – pin your colours to the mast. Scary maybe, but what a fantastic discipline!

So; you may say (as someone did to me only the other day) I really want to help my patient or the client I have been sent, but I really don't want to appear in court – that scares me senseless. Oh dear – this is the best bit! How can you tell me that you don't want to dress up in your Sunday best, travel vast distances, taking time off work (which you will need to make up later) and hang around a draughty waiting room for hours on end only to be torn apart by some smart-alec lawyer who has boned up on your subject only minutes before? Come on – you cannot be serious – this is what I live for! Okay I admit that court is not everyone's cup of tea, but believe me once you have been properly trained and prepared it really can be one of the most rewarding parts of the job and I really do love it! And if you have not been put off – you can read loads more about it later in the book. Even if you never acquire the taste there are some areas of practice where you are much less likely to have to attend – I will probably have to appear in a personal injury case the moment this book is published as some sort of divine retribution but believe me when I tell you I have not been once in twenty tears despite many last minute cancellations.

And if all of the above (never forgetting getting paid) is not enough reason for reading on, how about all those wonderful people you will get to know.

Do You Know a Good Expert? - Lawyers Tell Psychiatrists What They Want

Edited by Danny Allen

You may also enjoy the sequel – told by lawyers. Here is a taster:

Introduction – **John Wilkins**

There has been a great upheaval in the relationship between experts and courts, particularly in the Family Court arena. Never before has the spotlight been shone on so strongly on those, particularly medical practitioners and psychologists, providing expert evidence in the court system. The loss of expert immunity, the pressure on fees, the increased number of complaints made to the GMC and other professional bodies has led many to conclude that the work was more trouble than it was worth. This has led to difficulty in instructing experts particularly as experts become more conservative about the scope of their work. This will inevitably lead to poor justice for many and no justice at all for some.

It's a Shrinking Business

Following Danny Allen's previous book, told very much from the perspective of the expert, this volume comes as a timely reminder for those who are thus involved in expert evidence work of the issues involved, the frameworks used and perhaps, most helpfully the pitfalls that await the unsuspecting expert. Moreover, I am not aware of any other book that provides guidance and advice from the perspective of lawyers. It has always been my view that lawyers and doctors speak a different language, have a different way of approaching problems and therefore anyone who is intending to provide expert evidence has to understand the world in which lawyers work and the way in which our courts approach problems. This book is therefore timely and potentially helpful to anyone intending to embark on a career as an expert witness or even for those of us who have worked in the courts for many years.

Although the landscape in the criminal justice system has not changed anyway as near as much as it has in the civil courts and in particularly the Family Court, Maxine Cole's chapter provides a very useful description of the process taking a defendant from the point of arrest to court. This chapter will provide a useful guide for those unfamiliar with the criminal justice system. It also, usefully, refers to the Police and

Criminal Evidence Act (PACE), something that is often the focus of expert testimony.

Jon Nicholson's chapter on civil courts focuses, understandably, on personal injury. This is probably the area where most psychiatrists and psychologists will get involved in producing expert testimony and the chapter is a helpful digest of the fundamental principles affecting the civil courts and also provides useful reference materials. The basis of the Bolam Test, duty of care, causation and damages is particularly helpful as is the section on the joint experts report and I found it particularly useful to read the account of the rules and etiquette of talking to the different sides of the case, something that has exercised me from time to time.

The area where there has been most change over the past few years has been in the Family Court and Nadia Salam's chapter provides a useful explanation of the types of proceedings and the main players involved in any Family Court case. There is a useful explanation of the issues governing decisions made by the Family Court and what issues the court addresses when it is deciding about instructing experts. There is also a useful explanation of the scope of Family Court reports.

The thorny issue of medical records is addressed by Ali Malsher. Those of us who do expert reports are often frustrated by the lack of documentary information, the timing of the provision of medical records not to mention one's ability to read doctor's writing or decipher bad photocopying. There is useful guidance about what is expected of the expert in relation to medical records and what might or might not be relevant. I was reminded of the comment of a colleague of mine once, "Always read the papers!".

To anyone starting out on a career as an expert will want to know what to avoid in producing a report. Whilst Cyrene Aboy's chapter on this focuses on personal injury, it provides a useful basis for providing reports in any of the court forums. There is particularly helpful advice on the avoidance on the use of jargon, something that is second nature to most doctors and psychologists.

The book so far, having gone through the basics, then addresses some of the more subtle issues. Vikki Martin's chapter on the balance between evidence and opinion is particularly helpful. Again there is a very useful focus on what solicitors and courts expect from experts and perhaps most particularly what they do not want. Very useful tips on how to express an opinion and a further exposition of the Bolam test. The provision of a literature review is likely to become more common and will recall experts to pay attention to the scientific or evidential basis of their opinions. As an expert it is all very well to rely upon on one's own experience and expertise, but if it is possible to refer to peer review journals then all the better.

In addition to the changes in the Family Courts, the advent of the Mental Capacity Act has led to increasing requests for reports about an individual's capacity and Karen Shakespeare's chapter is again a useful introduction to what is expected in reports relating to mental capacity bearing in mind that this is a changing area of law. I found the template particularly useful but there are also useful tips for General Practitioners who will often get drawn into issues of capacity in relation to their patients as they are the ones that know them best.

Particular issues relating to the provision of neuropsychiatry reports are well covered in Megan Goodyer's chapter; this is particularly so in relation to issues of expertise. This is an area where it is easy for an expert to overplay their hand and portray themselves as experts when in fact they are not. There are further useful tips, perhaps the most helpful relating to the provision of draft reports. I have slipped up once or twice on this matter, to my embarrassment and discomfiture, when in the witness box.

One of the most contentious areas is in the provision of Family Court reports and particularly those relating to parents who are often being accused of abuse or neglect. Kirsty Richards' chapter provides a useful overview of how to deal with parents who are often hostile to the process and also provides useful tips in not overplaying your expertise and straying into questions of parenting ability which are most often the province of parenting assessments conducted by child health professionals and not experts.

Another area which has shown an increase in reports is in immigration cases. Leonie Hirst's chapter provides a very helpful description of the basics with a focus on the Human Rights Act, the Refugee Convention and also Immigration Detention. She provides helpful descriptions of tribunal procedures, the limits of expert testimony and also pitfalls to avoid. The potential basis for reports is also helpful for those who are perhaps doing these reports for the first time.

In Andrew Berk's chapter on employment reports, there is a good explanation of the effects of the Equality Act (previously the Disability Discrimination Act). This was the one chapter that also mentioned something that I considered to be important which is the frequently conflicting duty of an expert and the clinician who treats the patient. Although Andrew Berk does not exactly say as much, the implication is clearly that if you have a treating responsibility to a patient, providing an independent expert report is possible as the duties of an expert are primarily to the Court and the duty of care a clinician owes the patient according to the GMC guidelines are, in my opinion, incompatible.

One of the most daunting aspects of providing a report is having to meet the expert provided by the other side when there may be areas of disagreement. The chapter by Laura Millman and Katherine Pearce on experts' meetings gives useful guidance from the lawyer's perspective of what is expected from experts when they are trying to come to some sort of consensus document ,whilst also ensuring that they do not simply agree to avoid an appearance in court. If you are going to be an expert in court you have to have the courage of your convictions and be prepared to stand up in court and defend them. If you are not, then this is probably not the work for you. I can recall a colleague of mine who would never do reports for the civil courts and confined himself only to reports for the criminal courts purely on the basis that he did not consider himself temperamentally disposed to the often disputatious and hostile environment of a civil court hearing.

The simple adage of, "Stand up, speak up and shut up" is perhaps inadequate now as guidance for giving evidence in court. Shamsun Nahar's chapter on this is helpful and it reminds us of our duty to the court and not to the person that we have assessed or indeed the person who pays our bill. There is a useful guide in this chapter about dos and don'ts, which even thought I have given evidence many times over the years, I found useful and will probably keep as a reminder.

One of the major changes in the recent past has been the loss of expert immunity, something that seems to go back a very long time indeed. In fact, this chapter by Leslie Keegan provides a very interesting historical background to the question of expert immunity. None of us want to be sued ourselves and her advice about how to protect against being sued is again a chapter which is helpful to whether you are embarking on a career as an expert or have been doing it for many years. It also emphasises the issue of referring to a range of opinion. Your opinion may be entirely legitimate, but if there is an alternative opinion, which there often is in mental health, we are obliged to refer to it and to comment.

The trainee's viewpoint expressed by Sam Vhondo is helpful in the view of anyone coming to this work afresh. We are all aware of the situation where trainees see things with greater clarity and often ask questions which superficially seem naive, but which in fact are apposite. The section on the qualities that lawyers look for in experts is particularly helpful and again there is reference to confidentiality and conflicts of interest, something that tends to be overlooked at times.

The majority of experts providing evidence in court have not had accredited training for such work. Training schemes in general psychiatry, old age psychiatry and child and adolescent psychiatry do not have specific modules relating to providing expert evidence or indeed any aspect of medical jurisprudence. Most consultants have gone through a general training and their expertise is dependent upon their clinical experience and knowledge. The decision to provide expert evidence to the courts is usually a matter of personal choice or chance. It may be that a psychiatrist or psychologist is asked to provide one report in relation to a case and that report is well regarded enough for the firm of solicitors to ask that person to provide further reports in further cases and the clinician concerned gradually becomes 'an expert'. The name is quickly passed around between lawyers who ask each other, "Do you know a good expert?". Feedback from solicitors is rare and but in these days of revalidation for doctors we have to take steps to obtain feedback from them for appraisal purposes. Nonetheless, the most potent form of feedback is whether or not you are instructed again. It has been a reasonable assumption over the years that if you have a thriving medico-legal practice, you must be doing something right. However, that is probably not enough. Individuals who are want to give expert evidence now go on courses which, whilst helpful, provide a template that is particular to the trainer concerned and may not be relevant in all settings. For instance, a medical report that is suitable in style for the criminal courts, may not be suitable for the civil courts in a personal injury case. Experts have to be much more adaptable than they tend to be in the way that they write reports.

It is clear, therefore, that anyone embarking on a career as an expert or where they have fallen into giving expert evidence almost by accident need to look around for ways in which they can accrue the relevant expertise and knowledge in order to do a good job. If accredited training for such input does not exist or only exists for those who have had training in forensic psychiatry, and the courses that are provided by the legal firms tend to be idiosyncratic, books such as this can provide a very useful guide to what is required by the different branches of the legal system. I would recommend this book to all those who intend to start giving expert evidence, either by design or chance, and to those who are already providing expert evidence but want to do a better job particularly in the current climate of increased scrutiny of expert evidence in the justice system.

Chapter 1 - The criminal legal process - **Maxine Cole**

The objective of this chapter is to provide the reader with a basic outline of criminal procedure in England and Wales. Scotland is excluded because it operates under a separate legal system to that practised in England and Wales. We will be using the fictional case of R -v- John Smith, and 'travelling' with him through the criminal justice system where he encounters criminal procedure in action. Along the way we will examine other relevant cases. But first, what is criminal procedure? Simply put, it is the set of rules and practices that govern the way in which a person, called the defendant, travels through the criminal justice system.

A night to forget

John Smith is an ordinary 25 year old man, in an ordinary job, leading an ordinary life. On one of the nights in his ordinary life John went with his two friends, Peter and Mark, to a nightclub. Whilst inside, John became involved in an argument with a male, named Charles. The argument escalated into a fight between John and Charles, with his friends and others in the nightclub looking on. The police were called, but by the time they had arrived the fight had been stopped. John was being held by the nightclub door staff, whilst Charles was being tended to by members of the ambulance service. The police conducted enquiries and asked those present what had happened. They spoke with John and Charles, who gave their accounts. John stated that he acted in self-defence whilst Charles alleged that he had been assaulted by John in an unprovoked attack. John was arrested on suspicion of causing Grievous Bodily Harm (GBH) and taken to the local police station whilst Charles was taken to a nearby hospital. John's arrest as a consequence of the allegation made by Charles signalled his entrance into the criminal justice system; but first of all what is an allegation and what is an arrest?

The allegation against John and his subsequent arrest

An allegation is a statement made to police that an offence has occurred. On being told that a possible offence has been committed, officers are duty bound to investigate the allegation made to find out whether there is any substance to it. During the course of an investigation officers will interview the suspect and complainant, as well as speak with and take statements from witnesses.

They will also gather CCTV and forensic evidence, take fingerprints and photographs of the scene amongst other things. Now, whilst some allegations are deemed to be true such as the conviction, after trial of Costadinos Constavalos, also known as Dappy from the pop group N-Dubz (see R v Constavalos & others, 2012). Others, such as that made by Kirsty Debanks are clearly false. In Miss Debanks' case she told officers that she had been raped by her ex-partner Mr Newitt. Mr Newitt was held in custody for 6 hours but, fortunately for him, his alibi was corroborated by CCTV. This showed that Mr Newitt was elsewhere at the time of the alleged rape. So, on 17 May 2013 at Oxford Crown Court,

Miss Debanks, having earlier admitted to lying about the rape, was sentenced to 8 months imprisonment.

So, turning back to what Charles said to the police. He told them that John had assaulted him. This, being an allegation which clearly had some merit, given that Charles was bleeding heavily from his injuries, the officers decided to arrest John because the allegation was one of an arrestable offence; plus they have to obtain John's version of events in a formal recorded interview. Now the question arises as to what is meant by an arrest?

Although an arrest is the uttering of the words "I am arresting you….." and placing a person in handcuffs if necessary, officers have to be very careful when arresting a person. This is because they have "no more right to lay hands on someone than any other member of the community" (Parker LCJ in Ludlow & other v Burgess 75 Cr). So if they grab the person and then utter the words they can find *themselves* being lawfully assaulted as happened in Collins v Wilcox. In this case, an officer placed his hands on a prostitute to arrest her, however she punched him. She was later convicted of assaulting the officer in the execution of his duty, however appealed her conviction. On appeal it was held that she did not assault the officer in the execution of his duty because the officer, when he was assaulted, was acting outside the scope of his powers and thus did not have a right to touch her before uttering the words or informing her she was going to be arrested. The fact that, in response to his grabbing her, she punched him was deemed reasonable in the circumstances. There is, as you can see from this case a very thin line between a lawful arrest and an assault being committed by an officer.

So, turning back to our fictional case involving John, an allegation of assault has been made against him, as a consequence of which he has been arrested, and he feels the first touch of criminal procedure as he enters the criminal justice system. John is then placed inside a police van and driven to the police station.

At the police station

Once at the police station John is taken into the custody area. There he meets the Custody Sergeant who takes John's personal details and opens a custody record. This is a document on which his details are entered along with details of his personal effects, notes about medical conditions, demeanour, whether he is an illicit drug user or alcohol abuser etc. It also details the care that John receives whilst in custody and whether he has undergone any testing. For example, if John had been arrested on suspicion of driving with excess alcohol, then his intoximeter reading (the amount of alcohol in his breath) would be entered into the custody record. John is then placed in a cell to await the arrival of a solicitor or police station representative to represent him in the interview, but that is only if he wants representation.

John's representative is provided with initial 'disclosure' by the officer in the case. At this stage, the officers may only have preliminary details or evidence such as the initial complaint being handwritten and contained in the officer's notebook but they have to provide details of the offence being alleged. The interview is the time when John is asked for his account of events and can either provide a full account or choose to remain silent, only stating "no comment" and submitting a prepared statement in which he denies the offence alleged and asserts a defence or John could also decide to provide a mixture of the two. However, if he chooses not to answer any questions during his interview but provides an account at trial, the judge/bench hearing the case may, draw such inferences as appear proper from his earlier no comment interview (see s34(2) Criminal Justice and Public Order Act 1994).

At the end of the interview officers may decide to bail John pending the outcome of their further investigations, which could be to collect CCTV evidence or await results of forensics. Alternatively, they could decide that there is sufficient evidence with which to charge John with an offence. If the decision is that there is sufficient evidence to charge John then the police compile a file and present it to an Evidential Review Officer (ERO) for a decision. The ERO decides whether further investigative actions should be undertaken or whether the file should be passed to the Crown Prosecution Service (CPS) for a lawyer to authorise the police to charge John. The scope of the offences that police can charge people with are outside the scope of this chapter, but are contained within paragraph 15 of DPP Guidance (5th Edition, May 2013).

In John's case, the ERO decides that there is sufficient evidence to show that Charles' injuries and the circumstances amount to s18 Offences Against the Person Act 1868 Grievous Bodily Harm (GBH) and, as such, the file is passed to the CPS for a final decision. Meanwhile John is released from custody on conditional bail pending a final decision by the CPS.

It's a Shrinking Business

Bail

Bail is the procedural means by which people have their liberty removed, restricted or restored. When Bail is refused at the police station the person has to remain in custody under the Bail Act 1976 until they appear before a court. This is normally within 24 hours, hence the reason why specially selected courts are open on public holidays, to process what are known as 'custody cases'. Once in court the bail position is considered afresh. This can result in a person being freed entirely, only to return to court for their trial, sentence or administrative matters involving their case, or having their liberty removed and having to remain in custody, but at a prison. In John's case he has been granted conditional bail. This means that he is free to leave the police station but has to abide by the following conditions:

i. A curfew between 8pm and 7am – this means he must be at home from 8pm until 7am - if he is not then he risks being arrested and kept in custody until his first appearance before the court;
ii. Not to contact, directly or indirectly, the complainant, Charles

Plus, John must return to the police station on a fixed date and time where he will either be charged with an offence or informed that there is no further action to be taken against him at this stage. It should be noted that what has happened to John is not uncommon. We may consider, for example, the case of R v Philpott, Philpott & Mosley [2013]. This is a recent case where the parents and neighbour committed arson, killing six of the Philpott's children. All the defendants were placed on bail pending the CPS authorising the charges against them. But when they returned to the police station on their fixed date, they were charged and kept in police custody pending their first appearance before magistrates. They, however, did not apply for bail and were kept in custody throughout and so when they were sentenced on the 3 April 2013, they were somewhat used to their surroundings.

Charging

Once the police have sent their file to the CPS it will be reviewed by a Senior Crown Prosecutor who decides the level of the charges and produces a document of their advice and authorisation to charge called an MG3. The MG3 details the lawyer's reasons for authorising the charge by reference to the Code for Crown Prosecutors and the two tests:

i. Is there sufficient evidence to provide a realistic prospect of conviction?
ii. Is it in the public interest to prosecute?

Prosecutors must apply these tests and also consider any relevant case law, policy or guidelines before concluding that a person should or should not be charged. John's file is passed to the Crown Prosecution Service who, contrary to the ERO decision that it was a s18 GBH, has authorised that John is charged with s20 GBH contrary to the Offences Against the Person Act 1868; this is a lesser offence. They have also drafted the charge for the officer to put to John for when he attends the police station on his return date. When John is charged he was bailed for a second time, but this time he has added restrictions placed upon his liberty. On his bail sheet this time are two further conditions:

i. Residence at his parents address
ii. Not to go within 100 metres of the Ordinary Public House, in So So Lane.

It's a Shrinking Business

John's first appearance in court

The first court John appears in is the Magistrates' Court. Here he is placed in the dock and asked by the clerk to confirm his name and address. The clerk is a lawyer who sits below the bench where the magistrate sits. The clerk advises the lay magistrates and assists judges on points of law or other matters that may arise during the course of the court's business. It is quite a powerful position, the power of which Mr Munir Patel exploited to the full. Mr Patel was a clerk who dealt with traffic offences. In 2011 Mr Patel was sentenced to 3 years imprisonment for bribery and misconduct in a public office. What he had done was to accept payment for advice on how to avoid being summoned for traffic offences and prevented traffic penalties being entered onto the legal database.

The clerk then reads the charges to John and asks him if he wishes plead guilty, not guilty or to make no indication to the GBH offence. This is because GBH is an 'either way offence' which, means that it can be heard in either the Magistrates' Court or the Crown Court.

Although there are three options, what happens next falls into two streams. If John pleads guilty, the court is told the facts of the offence and the details of any previous convictions. They would then listen to any mitigation submitted on John's behalf by his representative. Having heard the facts and mitigation the court will proceed to sentence. The case may be adjourned for a pre-sentence report (by Probation) so that his personal circumstances and any sentence options can be examined including the possibility of his committal to the crown court for sentencing.

If John pleads not guilty or makes no indication, the court proceeds to *mode of trial*. Here the prosecutor presents the Crown's version of events and any other relevant factors. The defence also make representations but the Crown's case, at its highest, is taken.

The judge/lay magistrates then use what they have been told and the Magistrates' Court Sentencing Guidelines to decide which court should hear the trial (also known as deciding jurisdiction). If it is decided that the case should be heard in the Crown Court then the case is adjourned for committal. However, this procedure changed in 2013 and now the majority of cases should remain in the Magistrates' Court with only the most serious, or those at serious risk of receiving a custodial sentence, being sent to the Crown Court to be dealt with.

The issue of bail is also dealt with and, if the defendant is in custody, the clerk and prosecutor confirm the number of days left before which a trial must be held. Once committed John's next appearance will be at the Crown Court.

At the Crown Court

The indictment is read and the defendant is asked whether he pleads guilty or not guilty. If he pleads guilty he is sentenced either immediately or the case is adjourned for a pre-sentence report into whether the defendant has any issues. If these include drugs, alcohol or mental health problems, the report writer may request a psychiatric report. The pre-sentence report will also deal with the person's physical, or other, ability to carry out work.

If the plea is not guilty the matter is set down for trial. Directions are given that are essentially the timetable for certain events to take place such as the 'service of disclosure' and the response to the (prosecution) 'case statement' by the defence.

It's a Shrinking Business

About The Author

Danny Allen started his medical life doing house jobs in Kettering. After enjoying A & E and orthopaedics he rashly decided to become an 'orthopod'. After working as an anatomy demonstrator at St Marys, he toured the British Isles, failing his primary FRCS exams in some of the most scenic places in the land. After working as a GP in Australia, he decided to train as one and almost immediately did a year of ENT, which he loved and had to tear himself away from. After a spell in medicine and paediatrics in New Zealand, he did his trainee GP year in Basingstoke, but decided to do a spot of psychiatry before becoming a GP principal. Fortuitously, no 6 month jobs were available, so he was invited to join the local psychiatry rotation for a year, and has really never looked back since.

He was a senior registrar on the Bristol rotation before taking up a consultant post in general psychiatry in High Wycombe, where he spent a decade in a community mental health team before working in rehabilitation, assertive outreach, a crisis team and an acute day hospital. In 2005, in the intellectual equivalent of a mid-life crisis, he did a master's in mental health law at Northumbria University, which he thoroughly enjoyed. Although no academic, he has written over 20 papers on a range of topics. He retired from the NHS in 2011 and worked part time for a year doing substance misuse and psychiatry in an immigration removal centre; an experience which left him with very warm feelings - for the NHS.

From his time as a senior registrar, he has run a business providing medico-legal reports and, over the last decade, has worked with a group of associates to provide a comprehensive service to lawyers. He is now in private practice with a number of colleagues and continues to run his medico-legal practice. In 2012 he was elected a Fellow of the Royal College of Psychiatrists, brought out his first book: We Need It By Next Thursday - The Joys of Writing Psychiatric Reports and was elected chair of the Private and Independent Practice Special Interest Group of the Royal College of Psychiatrists. In 2013 he set up 'Professional Healthcare' a service for doctors and other senior staff providing general practice, mental health and occupational health care in one organisation and edited Do You Know a Good Expert? – Lawyers Tell Psychiatrists What They Want. He is also a Mental Health Tribunal member.

Bibliography

A Handbook for Expert Witnesses in Children Act Cases. The Hon Mr Justice Wall and Iain Hamilton. Family Law 2007

Assessment of Mental Capacity. The British Medical Association and The Law Society. The Law Society 2010

Business for Medics – How to Set Up and Run a Medical Practice. CreateSpace 2014

Do You Know a Good Expert? – Lawyers Tell Psychiatrists What They Want. Editor Danny Allen. CreateSpace 2014

Expert Psychiatric Evidence. Keith Rix. RCPsych Publications 2011

Faulk's Basic Forensic Psychiatry. J. Stone, K. O' Shea, Sarah Roberts, J. O'Grady & A Taylor. Blackwell Science 1999

Marketing for the Expert Witness. Catherine Bond and John Leppard. Bond Solon Publishing 1996

Writing Medico-Legal Reports in Civil Claims – an Essential Guide. Giles Eyre and Lynden Alexander. Professional Solutions Publications 2011

Professionals and the Courts. A Handbook for Expert Witnesses. David Carson. Venture Press 1990

The Expert Witness Marketing Book: How to Promote Your Forensic Practice in a Professional and Cost-Effective Manner. Rosalie Hamilton. Expert Communications 2003

The Little Book on Expert Witness Fees. Chris Pamplin. JS Publications 2007

The Little Book on Expert Witness Practice in the Civil Arena. Chris Pamplin. JS Publications 2007

The Little Book on Getting Started as an Expert Witness. Chris Pamplin. JS Publications 2008

The Expert Witness in Court. Catherine Bond, Mark Solon & Penny Harper. Shaw & Sons 1999

We Need It By Next Thursday – The Joys of Writing Psychiatric Reports. Danny Allen. CreateSpace 2014

Webography

www.archivebureau.com
Digital archiving

www.gmc-uk.org/doctors/revalidation/20386.asp
Suitable persons

www.hmrc.gov.uk
Tax and business

www.idf.uk.net
Independent Doctors Federation

www.medsu.org
Medical Support Union

http://doctorsappraisal.vpweb.co.uk/
Doctors Appraisal Consultancy

www.learn.bondsolon.com
Medico-legal training

www.moneyclaim.gov.uk
Online suing

www.ddc.uk.net
DBS checking

http://psychiatrycpd.co.uk
Going into private or medico-legal practice

https://drive.google.com
Google Drive

It's a Shrinking Business

www.callagenix.com
Computerised switchboard

Index

accountant, 12, 27, 29, 30, 32, 36, 75, 78, 83, 84, 90, 92
accounting system, 29
accounts function, 53, 59, 76
additional income, 30
ADHD. *See* Attention Deficit Hyperactivity Disorder
alcohol, 111, 129, 137
appeal, 128
arrest, 126, 127, 128
ASD. *See* Autistic Spectrum Disorder
Assessment of Mental Capacity, 141
associates, 84
Attention Deficit Hyperactivity Disorder, 18
Australia, 139
Autistic Spectrum Disorder, 18
bail, 131, 132, 133, 134, 137
Bond Solon, 19, 36, 141
bookkeeper, 53, 64
bottle of wine, 7
Bristol, 139
business, 2, 9, 10, 11, 12, 13, 21, 25, 27, 28, 29, 30, 31, 32, 41, 42, 43, 45, 47, 48, 50, 51, 52, 53, 55, 56, 57, 61, 64, 68, 71, 73, 74, 77, 78, 81, 82, 83, 84, 85, 96, 100, 108, 135, 140, 143
business plan, 31, 32, 93
Care Quality Commission, 16, 23, 47, 67, 75
CCTV, 127, 131
chambers, 18
Christmas card, 7
Citizens Advice Bureau, 68
civil procedure rules, 36
client, 23, 33, 44, 46, 50, 67, 110, 111, 112, 113
clinical psychologist, 111
clinical work, 108
community interest company (CIC), 78
competition, 31
complainant, 127, 132
conclusions, 112
Constavalos, Costadinos, 127
continuing professional development (CPD), 37, 71, 101
conviction, 127, 128, 134
court, 104, 106, 108, 112, 113, 132, 135, 136
CQC. *See* Care Quality Commission
CRB. *See* Disclosure and Barring Service
cremation form, 25
criminal, 104, 106, 108, 125, 126, 129
criminal justice system, 125, 126, 129

criminal procedure rules, 36
Criminal Records Bureau. *See* Disclosure and Barring Service
Crown Court, 127, 136, 137
custody, 127, 129, 131, 132, 133, 137
customer, 13, 49, 54, 59, 81
Dappy. *See* Costadinos, Constavalos
data controller, 33, 90, 94, 99
Data Protection Act 1998, 99
DBS. *See* Disclosure and Barring Service
Debanks, Kirsty, 127, 128
defence, 126, 130, 136, 137
defence organisation. *See* medical defence organisation
defendant, 125, 137
disciplinary and grievance procedures, 62
Disclosure and Barring Service, 66, 67, 143
Do You Know a Good Expert?, 4, 19, 115, 140, 141
doctor, 10, 33, 45, 76, 109, 113
Doctors Appraisal Consultancy, 76, 143
DX, 50
employer, 10, 12, 39, 40, 43, 63, 93, 98

Employers' Liability (Compulsory Insurance) Act 1969, 61
employers' liability insurance., 61
employing people, 30, 39, 61, 69
employment, 17, 22, 23, 29, 30, 43, 61, 78, 79, 112
employment lawyer, 69
England, 11, 125
ERO. *See* Evidential Review Officer
evidence, 127, 130, 131, 134
Evidential Review Officer, 131
expert, 104, 109
experts, 108
factoring, 55
family, 111
Family Court, 115, 116, 117, 120
fax, 49, 93
forensic, 25, 40, 104, 127
GMC, 10, 37, 52, 73, 76
Google Drive, 95
GP, 89, 93, 94, 95, 110, 139
Grievous Bodily Harm, 126, 131
Hallström, Cosmo, 8
hearing, 130
Her Majesty's Revenue and Customs. *See* HMRC
High Wycombe, 139

HMRC, 10, 28, 29, 31, 32, 36, 52, 63, 75, 90, 96, 100
hourly rate, 56
immigration removal centre, 140
imprisonment, 128, 135
Independent Doctors Federation (IDF), 76
Independent Financial Advisor (IFA), 36, 75
Information Commissioner, 33, 37, 90, 99
Information Commissioner's Office, 33, 90, 99
injury, 111
Institute of Directors, 24
interpretation, 2
interview, 127, 128, 130, 131
invoicing system, 29, 51
job plan, 12, 39, 40, 44, 89, 91, 97
judge, 27, 109, 130, 136
junior doctors, 105
Kettering, 139
Late Payment of Commercial Debts (Interest) Act 1998, 55
lawyer, 113, 131, 133, 135
limited company (Ltd), 78
limited liability company, 78
Macaulay, Andy, 101
Magistrates' Court, 135, 136

Magistrates' Court Sentencing Guidelines, 136
maintaining a good relationship, 59
Marmite, 103
MCOL. *See* Money Claim Online
medical defence organisation, 35, 37, 58, 89
medical director, 9, 89
medico-legal, 9, 10, 16, 19, 24, 35, 36, 37, 39, 40, 42, 43, 44, 45, 46, 50, 71, 72, 75, 76, 81, 105, 106, 107, 108, 109, 110, 111, 112, 140
medico-legal notes, 34
Medico-legal work, 7, 19
mental disorder, 109
Mental Health Act, 25, 26
Mental Health Tribunal, 7
Mental Health Trust, 7
mentor, 12, 37
mentoring, 105
Ministry of Justice, 21
mitigation, 136
money, 107, 108
Money Claim Online, 57
MP3 file, 50, 95
National Insurance, 63
N-Dubz, 127
neuro-psychiatrist, 110
New Zealand, 139
NHS, 10, 12, 15, 16, 18, 20, 23, 37, 39, 43, 44, 47, 62, 65, 66, 74, 75,

76, 79, 81, 85, 91, 97, 99, 100, 107, 140
non-geographical, 45
note of thanks, 7
occupational health, 140
offence, 127, 128, 130, 131, 133, 134, 135, 136
Offences Against the Person Act 1868, 134
Offences Against the Persons Act 1868, 131
orthopaedic surgeon, 139
P45, 64
P46, 64, 92
parents, 133, 134
passport, 64, 91, 92
password-protected, 33, 95
Patel, Munir, 135
patient, 20, 53, 56, 59, 66, 71, 77, 91, 94, 95, 104, 108, 110, 113
payment, 104
payroll, 13, 62, 63, 64, 68, 69, 75, 90, 92, 96
personal injury, 111, 114
Philpott, Philpott & Mosley, 133
planning permission, 16, 45, 46
PO (Post Office) Box, 47, 93
premises, 17, 35, 41, 46, 61, 77
pre-sentence report, 136, 137
principal, 84, 85, 139
Private and Independent Practice Special Interest Group, 140

private patient, 44
private practice, 10, 15, 18, 36, 39, 72, 87, 89, 92, 97, 100, 140
private psychiatric practice, 7, 8
professional, 12, 23, 33, 45, 48, 49, 51, 53, 56, 59, 65, 73, 79, 81, 82, 86
professional activity (PA), 23
Professional Healthcare, 140
prosecution, 137
psychiatric report, 137
psychiatrist, 9, 10, 15, 16, 17, 19, 22, 23, 24, 26, 40, 51, 53, 66, 74, 77, 78, 103, 109, 110
psychiatry, 104, 106, 107, 110
PTSD, 111
public, 108, 132, 134, 135
public liability insurance, 61
rape, 127
receptionist, 64, 65
records, 12, 52
referral letter, 97
renting, 17, 18
report, 104, 105, 106, 108, 109, 111, 112
responsible officer (RO), 76
rooms, 11, 17, 90
Royal College of Psychiatrists, 101, 140
salary sacrifice, 68
self-employed, 26, 30, 31, 90

senior registrar, 107, 139, 140
services, 2, 9, 18, 42, 44, 45, 47, 48, 49, 77, 90, 107
solicitor, 50, 53, 54, 56, 57, 68, 78, 84, 130
St Marys, 139
statement of truth, 36
Sudbury, Pete, 9
supervisor, 12, 37
tax compliant, 12, 59
tax investigation insurance, 36
taxman, 26, 27, 52
trainee, 139
trainees, 105, 111, 112
training, 104, 105, 110
trial, 127, 130, 132, 136, 137
tribunal doctor, 22
Trust, 37, 40, 41, 43, 45, 46, 90, 97, 99, 100
URL (uniform resource locator), 49
voice transcription technology, 43
We Need It By Next Thursday, 4, 19, 103, 140, 142
workplace, 12, 66, 112

Made in the USA
Charleston, SC
25 October 2014